Expanding Technologies—
Expanding Careers
Librarianship in Transition

edited by Ellis Mount

Special Libraries Association

**SPECIAL LIBRARIES ASSOCIATION
WASHINGTON, DC**

Expanding technologies--
expanding careers

The Economist Intelligence Unit
The Economist Building
111 West 57th Street
New York, NY 10019, USA
Telephone: 212-554-0600

SLA gratefully acknowledges the Economist Intelligence Unit, sponsor of the Nonserial Publications program.

© 1997 by Special Libraries Association
1700 Eighteenth Street, NW
Washington, DC 20009-2514, USA
1-202-234-4700
www.sla.org

Library of Congress Cataloging-in-Publication Data

Expanding technologies—expanding careers : librarianship in
    transition / edited by Ellis Mount.
        p.   cm.
    Includes index.
    ISBN 0-87111-465-8
    1. Information science—Vocational guidance—United States.
    2. Library science—Vocational guidance—United States.
    3. Information science—Data processing—Vocational guidance—United
    States. 4. Library science—Data processing—Vocational guidance-
    -United States.   I. Mount, Ellis.
    Z665.2.U6E97   1997
    020'.23'73—dc21
                                                                    97-16914
                                                                    CIP

CONTENTS

PREFACE

If one thing is certain about human endeavor, it is the fact that change is inevitable. Nothing seems absolutely unchanged through the years. In the case of employment and careers, we have come to expect different ways of doing things and new avenues to explore. Some of the new opportunities may turn out to be short-lived and literally worthless in the long run. Others, often viewed with skepticism at first, may quickly find worldwide popularity and genuine respect in all sectors.

Not surprisingly, the development of personal computers would head the list of many observers as the cause for new jobs. The influence of this invention is truly international, and new aspects of computer-based industries are constantly unfolding.

Once thought of as a novel but scarcely earth-shaking invention, even skeptics acknowledge that the world will never be the same as before the development of personal computers.

Consequently it should be not surprising that practically all of the alternative careers described in this book have some connection with the existence of computers and computer-based activities. The use of computers for online searching and creation of streamlined procedures has been well covered in recent years by books and periodical articles. These activities are hardly considered alternative nowadays. Comparing present-day conditions with those as recent as 1993, when another volume dedicated to alternative careers was published by the Special Libraries Association (1), it is probably not surprising that the word Internet never appeared once in that volume. The rapid growth in the world of information management shows how a major player in that world came into existence in four short years.

Thus it should be taken for granted that the chapters in this book show that current alternative careers consist of advanced, more sophisticated, uses of computers than those described in the book cited. Most of these positions required considerable study and independent mastery of new equipment and complicated processes. Often formal training and education was involved, but in many cases it was a case of finding local employees willing to share their expertise at the writers' places of business.

Aside from technical advances, it is apparent from reading these chapters that just as important is the person's skill in finding opportunities for advancement by creating new systems or by volunteering to take on more responsibility. The authors in this book are far from being shrinking violets—instead they are people who have confidence in their skills and are always on the lookout for new ways of doing things. Perhaps library schools will find ways of encouraging this sort of an outlook among their graduates—it was an obvious need for those who aspire to improve their status.

There are two main groups of careers in this book—those for entrepreneurs and those for employees. The entrepreneurs generally are people who have created their own companies, which they manage. The employees are those who work for others rather than be independent of supervision; however, many of them are supervisors of people or even whole departments in their organization. Their titles include manager, supervisor, or even vice president.

Each chapter follows the same general pattern: the writers describe their original training and early jobs, followed by analyses of what they do at their present non-traditional jobs. At the end of almost all chapters are discussions of what the authors feel would be helpful pointers on how to succeed in their present positions.

Two other chapters don't fall into either category. The paper by Jana Bradley consists of an analysis and brief survey of a number of innovative positions in the health sciences world. Many of the examples could just as well have been part of some other discipline, so the chapter should interest readers in other fields and professions. The second exception among the chapters was written by Jeanne Tifft, who examines the role of library education in helping graduates develop alternative careers, with comments on how she feels current curricula might be revised. Her own utilization of these techniques illustrates many of her points.

In reviewing a few examples of the contents of the volume, it should be noted that besides using modern technology, most chapters discuss activities commonly considered outside the scope of the traditional library, such as digitizing the syllabi at a university or creating databases for information accumulated by library users. Several authors have become consultants and found that they were involved in consulting with executives in major financial services or in government agencies. Others have become editors and compilers of publications such as financial newsletters or technical bulletins. Some chapters include accounts of authors who worked as consultants in foreign countries. Still others developed training courses they conducted for companies whose employees needed to update their skills in handling information. Several authors reported having written materials that were published as technical government documents or commercial software. Most of them found that the gaining of expertise in several areas of electronic hardware and software was indispensable for their careers. More than one person found that new technologies made it possible to be much more mobile in the conduct of business—they were freed from the necessity of working in their home base or of having to take large amounts of equipment and reference material with them when on the road.

It was a pleasure to work with the authors, whose cooperation was given willingly and promptly. It is hoped that this volume will make you more aware of the possibilities and the realities of alternative careers for librarians.

(1) *Opening new doors: alternative careers for librarians*. Washington, DC; Special Libraries Association; 1993. Edited by Ellis Mount.

Part One
Employees

CHAPTER 1

MANAGER OF A CORPORATE MEDIA ARCHIVE

KEVIN J. COMERFORD
Microsoft Corporation

INTRODUCTION

Intentions never seem to mean much in retrospect, but even so I still find it unsettling that all I intended to do after college was become a professional artist, and what it turns out that I have become is a special librarian at a computer software company. Growing up, I don't think I ever even considered librarianship as a career option, even though I have been fascinated with libraries and their assembled accoutrements (especially classification schemes) as far back as I can remember. In elementary school I recall that I had something akin to a religious experience when I finally figured out the main classes of the Dewey Decimal System. Still, it did not occur to me until much later that being a librarian was something I would do for a living. Not that I am complaining. I have had a stimulating career and have been able to do many more things with my life than would have been possible if I were simply painting canvases outside a grass hut in Tahiti.

My first experience actually working in a library was as an undergraduate student. As is the case with most art students, I was chronically short of money, opting to use what little I had for supplies. Once, after giving the school financial aid officer a particularly bad time about paying a late fee for an emergency loan (which was paid back 1 day late), I awoke the next morning to find an institutional work-study position referral pinned to my dormitory room door. Apparently I had made the financial aid officer sufficiently shameful about the loan penalty that he felt obligated to get me a job. The job, as it turned out, was as a circulation clerk in the university library, and I found I quite enjoyed the work, even though I was regarded suspiciously by the other work-studies who were majoring in respectable career fields. It seems that outside of the Art Department, art students tend to get a bad rap in the academic world, being characterized as mentally dull, lascivious, and generally unmotivated.

Hence, I had worked at the college library quite a while doing menial tasks before the work-study supervisor allowed me the privilege of typing new circulation punch-cards for the books. All-in-all it was not the type of positive experience that launches one headlong into a career.

After receiving my baccalaureate stripes, I taught art classes in various capacities and worked on preparing my painting portfolio for admission to graduate school. It was then that I literally stumbled upon a paraprofessional library position at the University of Texas, Arlington campus, by accident (after undergraduate school though, starving did not seem to be such an honorable calling as I had thought). I worked there a year as a circulation/reserves technician, and then while in graduate school at Texas Christian University worked another two years in both circulation and reference at that library. These jobs provided my first real introduction to librarianship as a profession, and sparked my interest in going on to library school.

While in art school at TCU, I also worked as a gallery supervisor, a junior college art teacher, a research assistant in Renaissance Art History, and in the art school slide library. All of these jobs together did not provide an adequate living wage, so during the summer between the first and second year of the MFA program, I attended my first semester of library school at the University of North Texas on a scholarship from the Texas Library Association. Unfortunately, this was the only period I was able to attend library school full time, and it subsequently took me six years to complete the MLS degree program on nights and weekends.

Upon completing the Master of Fine Arts degree, I went on to an internship in the Visual Resource Library at the Dallas Museum of Art. It was intended to be a one-year introductory program, but as it turned out, the department head resigned shortly after I began, and I found myself running the library alone.

NATURE OF THE WORK

The Visual Resource Library at the Dallas Museum of Art (DMA) houses a medium-sized collection of one hundred thousand, 35mm slides and two hundred fifty thousand prints and transparencies. When I arrived at the DMA, the image collections were housed in the basement, and a good portion of the collections were backlogged and inaccessible to patrons. The only catalog for the collection was a makeshift database that had never been fully implemented. In addition to maintaining the photographic collections, I was also responsible for administering the museum's "Rights and Reproductions" service. In short, this involved receiving and evaluating requests to publish images of the museum's collection of art and ethnographic objects. Every sizable museum has a person or department devoted to this function.

In the Fall of 1990, the DMA received a grant from the Mellon Foundation to update its collections management database system. The museum evaluated a number of database vendors and elected to implement ARGUS, made by QUESTOR Systems. The primary role of ARGUS was to automate the administrative functions of the museum registrar's office. The decision proved to be a boon to my visual resource library however, as at the time the system was installed, QUESTOR had also just released a slide and photograph library module. QUESTOR had also provided the museum with a digital imaging subsystem for ARGUS, which allowed scanned images to be previewed in any museum object or photograph database record. No one in the museum had any technical expertise with multimedia, so it was decided on a whim that the visual resource library would house the imaging equipment (and subsequently manage the imaging effort).

By today's standards, when multimedia computing is a fact of life for most librarians, these humble beginnings don't sound too exciting. However, at the time we implemented ARGUS, it was just beginning to be feasible for a small institution to maintain an image database on its own. In fact, I remember it as being a very uncomfortable time, because the DMA was the only institution of its kind to be mounting a digital imaging project, and videodisc recording was really at the height of its popularity. A number of large museums published videodisc catalogs of their collections in the late eighties and early nineties, and they all viewed digital imaging as an "unfriendly" and non-portable medium (so much for the Internet). I literally had visitors from other institutions scoff at my miniature scanning shop, and, to my chagrin, tell museum donors that there was no future in digital imaging.

Over the next three years, I worked closely with QUESTOR to develop the DMA slide library system from a fairly straightforward database into an extremely versatile library management tool. We implemented custom programming that dynamically retrieved object data from the museum side of ARGUS, so I could in effect "copy catalog" slide and photograph records. We also implemented the (then) newly-published *Art and Architecture Thesaurus* (AAT) in electronic form, making it directly accessible to users from within the database. As an offshoot of this project, QUESTOR developed a utility that would scan the AAT terms used to index photograph records and from them construct a unique classification number.

Cataloging and imaging the visual resource collections was undoubtedly the most stimulating work I did at the museum (I have found I am a cataloger and classificationist at heart), but in a small, highly specialized library setting, practicality demands that one not only perform technical service duties, but also reference, patron services, collection development, administrative duties, and committee work. As a result, I was never able to devote quite enough time to my most favored professional activities. It always seemed that I had to keep involved constantly in each area of work to continue making progress in the library, and to prevent the demons of stagnation and backlog from overtaking us.

As busy as I managed to keep myself, I found that I was constantly worried about the end product of our cataloging and imaging activities: who was all this data really going to benefit? The museum staff were my primary patrons, but I also had a good size public audience of researchers, educators, and students who would use our facilities. The larger our imagebase grew, the more apparent it became that the museum needed a public access strategy.

In this regard, I think fortune literally smiled upon me, for I was able to see the entire automation effort culminate in a unique public access project. In late 1993, the DMA opened a huge, new, three-story wing called the Hamon building, which effectively doubled the size of the institution. Half of the new building's second floor was devoted to an expansive educational area called the Education Resource Center. It included classrooms and new departmental areas for the visual resource library, the museum's bibliographic library, and the museum education department. To attract new patrons and use this space to the fullest possible measure, the museum also invested quite a bit of effort into designing new public programs and services. This was highly advantageous to my own cause, as the notion of providing "public access" to the museum's collection records had become a popular idea amongst the staff. Because of this, I was able to pitch the idea of a creating a computer-based learning center within the museum fairly easily. The rationale I presented was a simple one: that a natural outgrowth of our cataloging and imaging activities was a facility where this and other institutionally-based electronic data could be presented to the public.

I worked closely with the museum's Chief Operating Officer to develop the project, which I coined the "Collections Information Center." During this time I also worked in tandem with QUESTOR systems, who had developed a front-end module for ARGUS. The product had an OPAC-like interface and provided basic search capabilities (maker, title, subject), similar in look and feel to a bibliographic catalog system. The system would present the user with a catalog record, complete with digital images, for objects or photography owned by the museum. All of the elements for the Collections Information Center fell into place only a week or so prior to the Hamon building public opening. I learned to pull network cable, install network hardware and software, and administer a UNIX-based server all on my own to complete the effort on time. (This was not bad for someone who had no real computer experience until well into graduate school.) When the center opened, it was equipped with eight public workstations in sit-down carrels, a reference desk, and color printers to provide text and image printouts for patrons to take with them. Users had access to an image database of about 20,000 items (not all records had accompanying images), many with didactic essays or curatorial notes in addition to the basic catalog record. I managed several additional information technology projects at the DMA as well, one with CompuServe information service to provide a "Dallas Museum of Art" section of their Fine Art forum, another with a gopher and then a World Wide Web site on the Internet.

My work at Microsoft Corporation has been a fairly logical extension of my involvement with digital media resources. I joined the staff of Microsoft in July 1995 as Media Archive Manager, and my initial duties were to organize a collection of 10,000 video and data items in accordance with Motion Picture Association of America standards. My role has quickly expanded to include digital media.

My current duties focus on coordinating patron services and cataloging operations for the Microsoft Interactive Media Group. I am also part of an internal team that is developing a computer online media asset management system that will provide storage and retrieval for at least ten terabytes of media. My role in this effort has been to evaluate usability of the system, provide end-user training and support, and create media meta-data cataloging standards and practices.

Kevin J. Comerford
Media Archive Manager
Microsoft Corporation
One Microsoft Way, Red West A/1088
Redmond, WA 98052
Tel: 206/936-0528; Fax:206/936-7329
E-mail: kevco@microsoft.com

CHAPTER 2

LEADER OF LIBRARY INTRANET DEVELOPMENT IN AN AEROSPACE COMPANY

MICHAEL CRANDALL
Boeing Technical Libraries

INTRODUCTION

I arrived in the world of library and information science relatively late in life, after spending many years as an engineering geologist and a small business owner. Throughout both of these earlier occupations, I found myself fascinated by the central role that information played in the day-to-day activities associated with my work. As a geologist, the historical files of the company I worked for were a primary source of information for new projects, as was the publicly available research accessible through public and academic libraries and government agencies. The same was true as I explored and finally created the small business (a bicycle shop) that my wife and I ran for seven years in Washington State's San Juan Islands. Without access to information, neither of these endeavors would have been possible, let alone successful.

It was actually a book, Jeremy Campbell's *Grammatical Man* (1), that inspired me to return to graduate school and investigate the world of information more fully. While at the University of Washington, where I received my MLIS degree in 1986, I was fortunate enough to receive a National Science Foundation Fellowship to work with Dr. Raya Fidel on her study of online searching behavior (2). Through this work I became acquainted with the Boeing Technical Libraries in Seattle, Washington, and was offered a job there as a research librarian.

During my six years in that position, I became familiar with most of the common online services (and some rather uncommon ones as well), helped to develop a collection development policy for the libraries, and worked as part of a team that evaluated and defined the libraries' processes and products. These efforts later became the basis for the libraries' product strategies, and provided the foundation for many metrics used to track the libraries' quality improvement efforts (3).

NATURE OF THE WORK

My present job is leader of the Intranet Development Group in the Boeing Technical Libraries. The move to my current responsibilities was an evolutionary one, that parallels to some extent the growth in the use of electronic mail and the Internet both inside and outside the Boeing Company. Some background about Boeing, computing systems inside Boeing, and the Boeing Technical Libraries will help to set the context for my transition to intranet librarian.

Background

The Boeing Company is one of the largest aerospace companies in the world, with over 147,000 employees in multiple locations throughout the United States and the world. The business units and operating divisions within the company have historically developed their own information systems based upon customer requirements and internal needs. This has resulted in a diverse networking and computing environment, with virtually every major (and minor) manufacturer or vendor represented somewhere within the company.

Because much of the information on the company's networks is competition-sensitive, Boeing, like other corporations, provides a "firewall" around the company's computing systems that does not allow general access from the outside. Employees within the company have access to all authorized portions of the internal network, including the internal web and, where appropriate, access to the Internet and the World Wide Web through dedicated gateways or proxy servers.

The Technical Libraries at Boeing have traditionally been the focal point for distributing external information to Boeing employees. They also index and abstract the internal company documents into the online catalog system. A full-time staff of 44 people manages the collections and provides services to over 28,000 employees a year. The library has four separate geographic locations in the Seattle, Washington area, with smaller independent libraries in Philadelphia, Pennsylvania, Wichita, Kansas, and Huntsville, Alabama that share the online catalog system. The recent acquisition of Boeing North America (formerly a part of Rockwell International), and the potential merger with McDonnell Douglas may change this picture in the future, but this scenario is still unfolding.

Because of the wide geographic distribution of Boeing employees, many library services are provided remotely. A staff of 12 research librarians provide mediated access to online information resources, producing about 14,000 customized research packages for employees every year, along with 825 ongoing updates on specific topics for individual employees. Some 8,500 employees have accounts on the online catalog, which is currently based on an IBM mainframe platform and uses the internal SNA network for access. This system is being replaced by a UNIX-based system in the first half of 1997. Primary customer access will be via the Boeing Web.

The libraries also are the purchasing agents for publications distributed throughout the company, including electronic publications, and provide routing and direct delivery for newsletters, newspapers, periodicals, and reports used by employees at the various locations.

Electronic Delivery Services

Beginning in 1991, in response to employee requests and changes in the publishing industry, it became apparent that the Boeing Libraries needed to develop an automatic distribution system for full-text electronic publications. One of the primary groups I supported as a research librarian was also one of the most vocal requesters for this type of service. The Technical Libraries decided to use this group's request for electronic delivery of the *Commerce Business Daily* as a pilot project. The Technical Libraries were routing multiple paper copies of this publication to users throughout the country, and the time delay through normal routing was unacceptable because of the necessity for quick reaction to items contained in the publication (primarily requests for proposals for government contract opportunities). The publication averages over 30 pages of fine print per day, and only small (but varying) portions were of interest to each employee needing access to the publication.

Because I knew the customers well, and had become somewhat familiar with Boeing's computing systems and networks through earlier efforts to deliver bibliographies via the company e-mail system, I was given the responsibility to implement this system. A provider was found who could deliver the *Commerce Business Daily* in electronic format, and a license was negotiated for unlimited redistribution within the company.

After evaluating several information filtering products available at the time, TOPIC from Verity, Inc. was selected as offering the best performance and potential for future growth. The distribution mechanism was, by default, the company e-mail systems, which were the only paths allowing direct access to users in various locations on multiple computing platforms. This meant that the system was limited to ASCII text delivery only, since capabilities for image delivery and display varied from e-mail system to e-mail system.

Working within these constraints, an automated delivery system was set up to capture and redistribute the incoming electronic publication as it was received. Much of my work at this point involved building subject filters for each user, so individual employees would find only items of interest to them waiting in their electronic mailbox every morning.

As time went on, several other publications of major interest to the company were made available through this system. Some publications were also re-published internally on electronic bulletin boards. In many cases, substantial savings were achieved by consolidating smaller contracts, while allowing employees broader access to the information.

The major difficulties lay in convincing publishers to offer a blanket copyright license for the company at a reasonable cost, and working with publishers to develop their ability to provide electronic text as a replacement for paper copies currently being purchased.

The Boeing Web

In spite of these efforts to provide direct delivery of electronic information to our customers, the libraries still kept getting customer satisfaction surveys requesting direct access to information resources at the customer's desktop. In 1994, the first opportunity to provide such services across the company came with experimental installations of internal web servers at Boeing.

Working with the libraries' computing support organization, the Technical Libraries moved many of the full-text publications being distributed via e-mail to an internal website, and modified the e-mail distribution to work in conjunction with the web in January of 1995. My responsibilities now included designing and implementing the libraries' website, as well as continuing to provide services through the filtered e-mail delivery systems.

The Technical Libraries' early involvement in the Boeing Web, and presence as a primary content provider, meant that others throughout the company began to look to the libraries for assistance and guidance in helping the web to grow, and to develop company-wide tools to help use the Boeing web more effectively.

I became involved in projects to move the corporate information bulletins onto the web, and as a result helped to develop the internal company home page, which was hosted on the library web server. The libraries assumed responsibility for providing a company-wide index of websites, and began a basic subject classification system for important websites within the company (4).

A company-wide group to discuss information management issues on the Boeing Web was started by the library, and I now am responsible for arranging speakers and topics for this group. Most recently, the libraries have begun a pilot project to distribute real-time news throughout the company via the web and e-mail.

As these efforts grew in scope and diversity, additional staff was added by the libraries to help manage the projects and provide day-to-day support to customers. Much of my time now is spent working with customers to define requirements for new services, and with publishers to develop products to meet those services.

POINTERS FOR ACHIEVING SUCCESS

The success of the Boeing Libraries' efforts to move into the digital world is tied directly to involvement with the user community and responsiveness to their needs. As the web became more visible, our early efforts opened up opportunities to assume new roles in the company, and put the libraries in a leadership role within Boeing.

The most important qualification for a position such as the one I find myself in these days is a broad background in the theoretical underpinnings of librarianship and information science. Without an understanding of all the pieces involved in managing information and providing library service, there is a great danger in following a path that is too narrow, or worse, leads over a cliff. I am certainly not an expert in most of the areas I need to be aware of, but try to stay abreast of developments in the field by being involved in professional associations, attending conferences, and scanning literature and commentary from as many sources as possible.

The second most important skill needed is the ability to communicate with customers and suppliers. Much of what I do involves gathering requirements from the libraries' customers and translating them into something that makes sense to a publisher, and then communicating the publisher's needs and requirements back to the customers. This involves listening, synthesizing, and the ability to determine what makes sense technically and politically.

A close third is an understanding of the rapidly changing technology we all have to deal with these days. I will never be a computing or networking whiz, but I have made an effort to understand the jargon and the basics, because without this knowledge I would not know what is important and what isn't. It doesn't hurt to be able to figure out how to use common computing tools either— they turn out to be essential in helping get things off the ground sometimes. But along with this, it's important to know when to get expert help and pass the responsibility on to those experts.

Finally, and this is true for all jobs these days, it is important to be flexible and open minded. The world is changing rapidly, and solutions for today may not work tomorrow. New skills must be learned at the drop of a hat, and old ones must be changed to fit new ways of working. Be a sponge for ideas, and help others to understand and use them. Everything is complex these days, and solutions take many minds to develop, so watch, listen, and work closely with others.

Pros and Cons

The most obvious benefit of a job like mine is that it is fun— I enjoy learning new skills, meeting new people, and creating new things. There is much work involved as well, but it is always interesting and challenging. The opportunities for contact with leading-edge developers and publishers, involvement in a wide variety of roles within the organization, and work on first-time projects are endless. I have had the opportunity to do research with colleagues outside the company based on some of the systems developed in the libraries, and to publish articles and make presentations at conferences based on work that the libraries have done.

It is also rewarding to see the libraries being recognized throughout the company in new ways because of work that I have participated in, as well as to see new respect for the libraries' role in helping to manage and distribute information.

For someone interested in stability and constancy, work such as this would be a poor choice, but if you are looking for variety, stimulation, and a chance to be part of a rapidly evolving organization, I can't think of a better position to have than one related to electronic delivery of information in a special library.

REFERENCES

1. Campbell, Jeremy. *Grammatical man ; information, entropy, language, and life*. New York: Simon and Schuster; 1982. 319 p.
2. Fidel, Raya. *Extracting knowledge for intermediary expert systems: the selection of search keys*. Final report. Washington, DC: National Science Foundation. Div. of Information Science and Technology; 1988 June. 124p.
3. Campbell, C. A. Product service strategies for information services. *FID News Bulletin*. 46 (4): 126-129; 1996 Apr.
4. Crandall, Mike; Swenson, Mark C. Integrating electronic information through a corporate web. *Computer networks and ISDN systems*. 28: 1175-1186; 1996.

Michael Crandall
Boeing Technical Libraries
P.O. Box 3707, M/S 62-LC
Seattle, WA 98124-2207
Tel: 206/237-3238; Fax: 206/237-3491
E-mail: mike.crandall@boeing.com

CHAPTER 3

INSTITUTIONAL RESEARCHER

ANN M. DeBIAK
Arizona State University West

INTRODUCTION

One of the great curses of my life has also been one of my greatest joys: I am interested in absolutely everything, albeit to some lesser or greater extent. An interest in everything is a considerable drawback when looking at future occupations and courses of study; it is a considerable asset if one falls into a job involving what is generally termed "institutional research." I am being quite specific in using the phrase "falls into," because that is what has happened to every person I have ever met in this profession. No one plans to go into this field, but once there, no one wants to leave.

I originally started work on an unpaid basis as a programmer for the University of Calgary in Calgary, Alberta, Canada, while I was in high school. Those were the days of teletype machines and keypunch cards. Basically, our "Computing Club" at the high school was given a free computer account at the university so we could hack and crash the system when modifications were made; to provide programming support for university class projects; and to create computer games for the annual university open house. Computers have been in my blood ever since.

My interest in the sciences and my computer background enabled me to obtain a paying job processing and analyzing geophysical data in the oil patch. Back then, as is the case today, there are limits on career advancement without that academic piece of paper. So, I attended the University of Western Ontario in London, Ontario. I had intended to get a business degree, but instead found myself fascinated by economics and medieval history. My hire as a research assistant to one of my history professors gave me my first taste of the primary components of institutional research: raw data and statistical programming. Given the limited job opportunities available in medieval economic history, I spent a number of years in the family retail trade and chaired several business committees. I eventually decided that library and information science offered the perfect climate for my diverse interests and abilities. I received an MLIS from the University of Western Ontario in 1991.

I have only had two traditional library positions, and even they were not all that traditional. The first was as an assistant to the school librarian in my junior high school. She used me as a filter and guinea pig for new book purchases. I was twelve.

My second position was as a records manager for the Ice Centre and for the Ice Reconnaissance Division; both branches of the Atmospheric Environment Service for the Canadian government. The title was really quite a misnomer as the position was actually that of a librarian for special collections. This position was obtained as part of a work study program while I was an MLIS student. During a span of eight months, I standardized the cataloging and classification procedures; created a combined classification code and authority file database; and restructured the classification system to be both expandable and hierarchical.

I made two important discoveries while in library school. First, I did not want to be a librarian. I had very much enjoyed my sojourn at the Ice Centre, but opportunities such as that were few and far between in the real world. I had no desire to answer directional questions at a reference desk or to sit cloistered in a back room cataloging. Second, was the realization that information science with its emphasis on the nature of knowledge and its partnership with technology was ideal for me. My degree in information science provided an appropriate piece of paper and level of diverse expertise needed for my first real foray into institutional research. I became the research officer for the Langley School District in Langley, British Columbia. After four years in Langley, I accepted a position as a planning analyst for Arizona State University (ASU) West in Phoenix, Arizona.

NATURE OF THE WORK

What is "Institutional Research?" Institutional researchers seem to spend a lot of time trying to explain to themselves and others just what it is they actually do. Definitive descriptions are difficult because the expectations and institutional constructs all vary so widely. Generally speaking, the role of an institutional researcher is to transform data into information, which can then used by the institution's constituents for making informed decisions. Additionally, the institutional researcher can take on a proactive role in the organization by being a catalyst for change. An institutional researcher is in the enviable role of not only having access to detailed data on the organization, but also has the technical expertise and understanding of the data so as to bring important analyses and concepts to the attention of decision makers.

The job titles among institutional researchers vary widely. At ASU West we are generally called planning analysts, although the next budget redefines my particular position as an assessment coordinator. Some institutions call us institutional researchers or analysts, some emphasize assessment, evaluation, and accreditation, and others include budgeting or policy analysis designations.

The variations in job titles are a reflection of the diversity of the backgrounds and expectations of people in this profession. This was one of the reasons for a study done by the Association for Institutional Research (1996) to discover who we are. The study found that, unlike librarianship, the gender split among institutional researchers is quite evenly distributed; 54% male and 46% female. Most people in this field have a doctorate (50%) and 38% hold masters degrees. But what is especially interesting is that although institutional researchers usually work for post-secondary institutions, only 15% hold degrees in higher education. The people I have worked with have degrees in psychology, public administration, computer science, and economics. Strangely enough, the study did not mention library or information science as common degrees in institutional research. Strange, because institutional research suits well the temperament, aptitudes, and training of many librarians and information scientists.

The Langley School District

The Langley School District is unusual in several ways. First of all it is quite large. The student body consists of approximately 20,000 students and there are about 1,800 full-time and part-time staff, but it is not an urban school district in the traditional sense. There is a city core, but the school district covers an area of nearly 104 square miles, much of it agricultural. Some of its metropolitan flavor comes from its proximity to Vancouver. It is also one of the few school districts in Canada that uses a decentralized system of administration among its 34 elementary and eight secondary schools.

As a result of the diversity among its student body and its decentralization, whereby budgeting and other decisions are made primarily at the school level, a system of assessment and evaluation evolved. The title of research officer at the Langley School District meant exactly that:

if any sort of research was required, I was given the project. However, budget evaluation was conducted by the District Administrator for Planning. As research officer, I designed and administered a rather remarkable array of survey instruments to all of our students older than seven years; to all the staff, faculty, and administrators; to members of the local community; to parents; and to our alumni. The coursework I had taken in research methodology and statistics in undergraduate history, econometrics, and in my MLIS program, proved invaluable.

Surveys comprised about 40% of my job responsibilities. The surveys were designed to be primarily multiple choice response to enable them to be printed on machine scannable forms. Unfortunately, open-ended questions could not be scanned and therefore the connection between open-responses and other responses, including demographics, was lost. The scanning, analysis and reporting required the use of a wide variety of software; scanning, word processing, spreadsheets, graphics, and database programs.

Another 10% of my position also drew upon my experience and training in research methodology and survey design. Individuals working on their masters and doctorates would often contact us, wanting to use our students and/or staff as subjects for their research. As a result of these numerous requests I was given the opportunity to design a policy for external research proposals. Research proposals were evaluated according to carefully determined criteria. I would like to think that the recommendations I made to researchers for modifications to their instruments and research design helped them to produce a better thesis.

But, "research" was defined very loosely in the Langley School District. In addition to taking on the production of our annual report, and becoming proficient in using Photoshop, Pagemaker, and the general rules of desktop publishing, I took on a very unusual task. I have never encountered other researchers who have been assigned this duty, but it is perhaps the most important and most difficult thing I did in Langley. I interviewed children regarding allegations of child abuse perpetrated by school district staff. The school district administration took the welfare of its students very seriously. Every allegation, no matter how preposterous, was investigated thoroughly and fairly to all parties concerned. So, I "researched" child abuse cases under the tutelage of a very adept lawyer. Remember the "tricks" and techniques you learned during your MLIS program on how to conduct a good reference interview? Well, they can be applied to a lot more than reference questions.

Arizona State University West

After four years in Langley, in Fall 1995, I accepted a planning analyst position at Arizona State University West. ASU West is part of the Arizona State University system, but is separately accredited. ASU West is what is referred to as an upper-division university. This means that although ASU West confers bachelor and master degrees, it does not offer coursework at the freshman or sophomore levels.

Many of my responsibilities as a planning analyst are similar to those in Langley, with the exception of investigating abuse allegations. As important as those investigations were, I do not miss doing them. My primary responsibility at ASU West is survey construction, administration, analysis, and reporting. It is due to the concentrated amount of time I spend on surveys and other assessment tools that my title is being reclassified as that of an assessment coordinator.

Surveys are becoming increasingly important in post-secondary institutions as universities and colleges are having to prove to their students, legislatures, accrediting bodies, and communities that they are providing the services and educational opportunities expected of them. The push to assess the institution as a whole has also inspired individual departments and colleges to evaluate themselves and their role within the university and community at large.

Surveys are but a single example of how important it is for an institutional researcher to keep apprised of technological developments. The advent of reliable OCR technology and affordable duplex scanners has made it possible to scan not only multiple response questions, but also allow for entering open-ended responses onto the same record simultaneously.

My position does not limit me to surveys, however. I am still able to utilize my desktop publishing skills in creating our institution's fact book. A university fact book, or statistical summary, is a document containing data in the form of tables, charts, and graphs. A fact book is basically an institutional ready reference document. Our department is looking forward to putting our next fact book on the web.

My position allows me to continue to develop my skills on our mainframe, programming in SPSS and SAS, and "ftp-ing" data hither and yon. I have the opportunity to use mapping programs to assist in our institution's enrollment management efforts, as well as create and manipulate relational databases. I am encouraged to scout out websites and journal articles to discover environmental changes that may impact upon us, and to create and examine models of what is happening at other post-secondary institutions.

So, broadly defined, my position involves the coordination, design, and implementation of research/analysis projects in conjunction with administrators and faculty to meet institutional and departmental needs for strategic planning, assessment, and management. This in turn means that I get to work with cutting edge ideas and technology on diverse subjects and unusual perspectives, with people from assorted backgrounds and viewpoints.

POINTERS FOR ACHIEVING SUCCESS

My first algebra teacher, Mr. Lewis, told our class two very important things: 1) girls can do anything boys can do, and 2) numbers are magic. If you do not believe in the magic, mystery, and excitement of numbers, institutional research may not be for you. If you do not believe in his second point, you are limiting your opportunities for professional and personal growth in a much broader arena. In general, institutional researchers are individuals who are fanatically detail-oriented, interested in diverse subject areas, are well versed in a broad range of computer software and systems, and are intrigued by data and the implications of it all. Institutional research involves the taking of many puzzle pieces, from seemingly different pictures, and putting them together into a meaningful whole. The result is not unlike a surrealist painting by an M.C. Escher, which is a melding of art, mathematics, and altered perspective. It is the ability to create such a melding, and communicate it, that allows the researcher to be a true catalyst for institutional change.

As in any occupation, communication skills are of extreme importance. In institutional research, as at the reference desk, listening well is the most important part of communicating well. The training librarians receive in conducting reference interviews is invaluable when dealing with clients in the institutional arena.

I have friends from library school who are still trying to convince me that I have a future in libraries; I tell them they can have a future in the creation of information not just the organizing of it.

For more detailed information on institutional research check out the web pages for the following.

●AIR (Association for Institutional Research) at www.fsu.edu/~air/home.htm.
●SCUP (Society of College and University Planners) at www.scup.org/.
●AERA (American Educational Research Association) at aera.net.

Another useful research page with links to a variety of sources is apollo.gmu.edu:80/~jmilam/air95.html.

There are many other websites that cater to the needs of institutional researchers that can be found using any of the major web search engines.

Ann DeBiak
Senior Planning Analyst (MC0651)
Arizona State University West
Institutional Planning and Research
PO Box 37100
Phoenix AZ 85069-7100
Tel: 602/543-5101; Fax: 602/543-5950
E-mail: adebiak@asuvm.inre.asu.edu

CHAPTER 4

MANAGER OF COPYRIGHT AND ELECTRONIC INFORMATION

Timothy J. Edwards
National Ground Intelligence Center

INTRODUCTION

When I entered the MSLS program at Catholic University of America I heard the term "retread" applied to a human being for the first time. Actually, most of us were in second, or even post-retirement careers. In my case, the cold reality that there were very few teaching positions available that would make the Ph.D. I was working on worthwhile sunk in. Since I was working part-time at Alderman Library at the University of Virginia, and received some timely advice from a mentor ("You're good at this, Tim. Why don't you consider a library career?"), and also received a bit of money from the university, I took the veil. I haven't looked back, but I have done precious little "traditional" library work since. Let's look at some traditional and not-so-traditional training that has helped me tremendously.

The MSLS at Catholic University followed classic lines. However, I had the benefit of some professors who encouraged us to think outside the boundaries. Those professors often talked of the politics of librarianship as opposed to simply customer services, or technical services. The politics of librarianship had to do with working through the organizational structure in order to perform as a librarian. It involved producing documents that captured the attention of powers-that-be, which involved good writing skills. Good writing is like good story telling: A lie well told can be enjoyable, but the truth well told is a thing of beauty. My own experience in a Ph.D. program had buttressed my writing skills considerably, but even then I relied on a practical little book that stressed the importance of clarity, connecting sentences, and careful proofreading to crafting a good piece of writing. Perhaps more than anything, the focus on good written communication at Catholic University has helped me live outside the classical lines of librarianship quite comfortably. The emphasis on not-necessarily-library-skills led me to pursue other training once I arrived in my present position at the U.S. Army National Ground Intelligence Center, formerly Foreign Science and Technology Center.

NATURE OF THE WORK

Whatever one may say about the Army, they are never short on training opportunities. Some examples of the type of training that help tremendously when one is put in a non-traditional library situation are Team Building, Personnel Management for Executives, and Organizational Leadership for Executives. These courses dealt with supervision and management issues, but, more importantly, were geared toward helping one understand the organizational structure within which one works. Further, these courses emphasized interpersonal relationships in both immediate and external work situations. Finally, training in funding cycles, and contract management is invaluable when charting or re-charting a program. In other words, each organization will offer training in how to understand the structure, lines of communication, and money management of that organization.

A librarian should take advantage of every opportunity that offers insight on how to achieve goals. The fact is, the idea of attractive visibility works wonders in dealing with the folks that make the final decisions on where to spend the organization's money. This is not a sell-out to management, nor a personal affront. If you're serious about where you want to go with your job, get the best map available. Often that map is offered within the work place through formal or informal training on the organization itself. More often than not, a non-traditional library position will require such training as we have mentioned, and more, even though on the surface it may appear to be a run-of-the-mill librarian position.

My job description looks like a U.S. government employee at the GS-1410-13 series and grade level. In other words, it includes such things as collection development, acquisition, customer service, and bibliographic instruction. However, the interpretation of those traditional terms into my everyday job is fueled by much necessity and a bit of ingenuity. In order to understand the method to this madness, it is necessary to view a job description as a frame work within which many functions may occur. If all we have is the framework, the job structure will be far too rigid to allow for the flexibility necessary to perform the tasks of librarianship in a non-traditional setting. The U.S. Government Library series standards (GS 1410, 1411, and 1412) were updated in 1994 by the Office of Personnel

Management (OPM), but the previous standards were written in 1966. The new standards allow and encourage flexibility within a traditional library job description, but the incumbent and his/her supervisor must address the actual requirements of the job in a non-traditional library in order to make full use of the OPM standards.

For example, the following are some of my duties.

1. Facilitate the development and acquisition of electronic resources through dialog with data providers and information technology personnel. In other words, create and maintain good working relationships with in-house computer specialists and external data vendors so as to make sure each purchase is a proper interface and not a waste of the next item.

2. Interface with budget officials in preparation and execution of budget and acquisition processes. This simply requires a knowledge of where to go with your questions on how to purchase something for the library. Then, follow the instructions. Unless you are one of those fortunate few who are blessed each year with more budget money than you can spend, this is not as traditional as it looks.

3. Write justifications and impact statements for unfinanced requirements, in order to procure non-budgeted items or begin new projects. This requires convincing a total stranger two hundred miles away to care about what I want to do! And, frankly, it is not a normal human function.

4. Develop policy, procedures, and a database that will ensure compliance with existing copyright laws. Negotiate blanket copyright agreements with information providers that will reduce most of the paper work involved in requesting permission to use copyrighted material.

5. Interface with customers on most anything you might imagine. We once received a request for the name of Annie Oakley's horse!

6. Other duties as assigned. (Everyone's favorite!)

Perhaps if I described a few parts of my job in a less formal way, it might be more clear to you. For example, part of my duties consist of trying to set up blanket copyright agreements with periodical publishers, which involves arriving at prices for photographs to be used in electronic publications. One complication is that the publications themselves do not have much in the way of precedents on how to arrive at pricing such materials. At the same time I must make sure that NGIC complies with existing copyright laws in negotiating blanket copyright agreements.

Another duty of mine is to write documents that present the needs of NGIC for funding or project initiation. I'm dealing with some unknown official in some distant location about our local needs.

POINTERS FOR ACHIEVING SUCCESS

Finally, saying what we do, and doing it are different animals altogether. I will conclude with some thoughts (all mine, but tenderized by training and experience) on what it takes to succeed in a non-traditional library setting.

1. **Flexibility**. I've been reorganized three times in six years (supervisor to non-supervisor to branch chief to non-supervisor). If you take a narrow view of what your job is, regardless of whether you are afraid of being taken advantage of, you will not be in a position to do some pretty exciting things. Cultivate a broad view of your job situation. Who is affected by it? What might be the outcome if, suddenly, you were placed in an entirely new job? What librarian skills can be adapted to most any situation? You might be surprised at how easily your skills carry over from one area or field to the next. However, flexibility must be cultivated personally.

2. **Trained Management**. Your management chain must be trained to expect you to come through in a pinch. Too often, I hear that we librarians are being "dumped on." Is that true, or is it because management has confidence that we can handle most anything that comes our way? Look at what management is sending you. If nothing new (as in new technology, or new programs) is coming your way, start training your management chain. That is, let them know or see that you can and should be involved in new developments and ways of doing things. Most librarians, traditional or not, live somewhere between the technological pioneers and the "gimme-paper-or-gimme-death" crowd. We serve many types of customers, and they all want results yesterday. They, too, can be "trained."

3. **An Open Mind**. Much of what we do leads to divergent paths. Look down the untrodden path sometime. Relying on past methods or techniques would never bring success in many of my daily tasks. I must be able to assess the wisdom of the means of accomplishing what I'm working on, regardless of whether or not I had ever used that particular procedure before. In other words, having an open mind is one absolute requirement for my job.

Timothy J. Edwards
Librarian
National Ground Intelligence Center (NGIC)
220 Seventh St. N.E.
Charlottesville, VA 22902
Tel: 804/980-7514: Fax: 804/980-7510
E-mail: tjedwar@ngic.osis.gov

CHAPTER 5

MANAGER OF A COMMERCIAL INFORMATION BROKERAGE FIRM

MADELINE J. KIELY-ENG
Moody's Docutronics Information Services

INTRODUCTION

My present position is vice president of Moody's Docutronics Information where I am the senior executive of this unique unit of a department within Moody's Investors Service. The events that led to my being chosen to head this organization are a good example of the alternative careers open to those who have been trained as librarians.

Most of my working career has been as a special librarian in the field of business and finance, but, like many of my colleagues, librarianship wasn't my first career. My first degree was a Bachelor of Science in Physical Education, then a Masters of Science in Recreation Therapy & Adapted Physical Education. My first jobs involved recreation therapy and adapted physical education. It was a far cry from my present position, but I've found that I take a coaching approach to supervising and directing my staff, which has stood me in good stead as a manager of a major business unit.

My first job as a corporate librarian began in 1984 at BEA Associates (now a Credit Suisse company) where my predecessor, Anita Collins, gave me a crash course into the mysteries of special librarianship within a portfolio management firm. I found that the founder and then president of the company, Albert Zesiger, fostered a progressive and forward thinking environment, which I came to appreciate as I moved on to other positions.

Four years later I went to Financial Guaranty Insurance Company (FGIC), where I established a records management program and managed the Information Center, which enabled me to hone my database searching and research skills. Next I moved to First Manhattan Consulting Group (FMCG) with the title of Director of Research. I reported directly to the president of the firm, Jim McCormick, a visionary in the fields of banking and management consulting. It was here that I learned how to turn a corporate library from a department that had always operated as overhead into a department that was a profit center. More importantly, I learned how to operate and thrive in an entrepreneurial environment: the founding partners were originally McKinsey & Co. and Booz Allen consultants.

It was while I was working at FMCG that I decided to earn a Masters in Library Science at St. John's University, a process that took four years of night classes. Having an incredibly supportive husband, Herbert Eng, made this achievement possible. Each semester, twice a week, he'd pick me up at the train station after work, drop me off for class, and then pick me up, bring me home, and provide me with a hot meal! What made his commitment to my career—and me—all the more amazing and wonderful is the fact that halfway through this arduous process we found that he had a serious illness. When I wanted to withdraw from my courses and the program, he insisted that we continue as though nothing out of the ordinary had occurred. I obtained my MLS degree in the spring of 1994, and Herbert died on June 30, 1995.

I left FMCG when an executive recruiter told me of a position at the Boston Consulting Group (BCG). I took the job for the opportunity it presented in being called upon to develop a library for this leading organization's New York branch office and then work within its topflight worldwide special library system.

Once the corporate library was firmly established, I moved to Moody's Investors Service, where I managed the Public Finance Information Center for three years. This was my first experience directing a large staff-- approximately 35 individuals at one point. From there I was recruited by The Estée Lauder Companies Inc. to establish a virtual library mandated to support all of its brands in new product development, sales, and marketing. I was given the title of Director, Business Information Center, with the responsibility of also serving other corporate departments— strategic planning, legal, research & development (R&D), and investor relations. Once on board, my role expanded to include directing operations within the advertising archives, further broadening my experience in supervising the handling of archival materials.

In the spring of 1996, when the founder of a unit of Moody's Financial Information Services (F.I.S.) decided to leave in order to pursue other interests, I was recruited back to Moody's to head this operation that

Moody's had acquired a little over a year before. I chose to take on this larger challenge and risk of running my own profit and loss division and become the senior executive in Moody's Docutronics Information Services with the official title of Vice President, Document Retrieval & Research.

This advancement into the level of being an officer of a prestigious company was an exciting event, one that I had never actually envisioned as possibly happening to me. Yet I could see that each of my former positions was actually a step forward, preparing me for this opportunity. In retrospect, I was never job-hopping, rather, I was always building my career and designing the next step in my life.

NATURE OF THE WORK

Docutronics provides current or historical international information on-demand and specializes in all information brokering practices that support strategic planning, market analysis, mergers & acquisitions (M&A), the acquisition of competitive data, legal inquiries/trial support, compensation reviews, and more! We are experts at gathering anonymous and corporate intelligence, as well as establishing both manual and electronic (Selective Dissemination of Information: SDI) current awareness services such as clippings, watches, and monitors. We are strategically located in offices in New York and Washington, DC, and our clients include many Fortune 500 companies, as well as the top investment banks, management, consulting, law, and advertising firms.

A typical day for me can consist of strategic planning, report or presentation writing, directing the operation and staff through my management team, managing the budget, and solving any problems that might arise throughout the course of any given day. Most recently I have been working closely with our marketing group to develop new products and aggressive advertising and direct mail campaigns. Does "Outsource to the Smart Source" sound familiar?!!

It's important to join, be actively involved, and sponsor special events for the pertinent information professional trade associations. I myself was on the New York chapter of the SLA's Business and Finance Division's Audit Committee for a number of years and chaired this committee in my third and final year. I was also an active member of my chapter's committee to determine, coordinate, and fund our topical monthly meetings. Each year, Docutronics, along with Moody's F.I.S. 's Sales & Marketing units, funds special events, scholarship funds, and local chapter meetings for key trade associations. Moody's party at the annual SLA Conference is known for being an event not to be missed!

POINTERS FOR ACHIEVING SUCCESS

To be successful as the head of a large information brokerage firm, one needs to develop a strong mastery of the principles of special librarianship and information science, particularly database design and management. Understanding finance and accounting principles is also absolutely essential. You should be monitoring technological advancements on an on-going basis, particularly as they relate to computers, telecommunications, and the ever-evolving Internet. One must become and remain, at the very least, a sophisticated end-user!

Strong communication skills in both the written and spoken word are necessary to support report writing and presentation development. The ability to travel a bit throughout the year in order to attend conferences, trade shows, and visit important clients must also be considered. A strong understanding and respect for the federal laws governing copyright issues, as well as all matters pertaining to confidentiality, are critical to success.

Finally, one must be detail oriented and have a passion for excellence. There should be a willingness and ability to work long hours and a driving desire to track down the most esoteric piece of data. Possessing an entrepreneurial spirit and strong inter-personal skills are essential elements as well. Finally, the ability to recognize proficiencies in others, and weaknesses in oneself, will afford you the ability to find the right mix of talent for your organization.

Every associate within Moody's F.I.S. department recognizes and appreciates librarians as their most influential and important customer base. Unfortunately, in our more expanded role as an information broker, Docutronics stands the risk of being perceived as a threat by corporate librarians in this age of outsourcing. We at Docutronics, and throughout F.I.S., are very aware and sensitive to this concern. We want to be a safe harbor and support service for information professionals throughout the world along with their sponsors. We would never consider circumventing corporate or legal librarians, thereby undermining their role within the organizations that they represent.

Some days more than others I feel the great responsibility that I owe to my company, staff, and internal and external clients. Yet despite all of the enormous pressure to keep Docutronics profitable and increase its revenue each year, I welcome all of the challenges and look forward to serving our clients' information needs in this age of the virtual workplace.

Madeline J. Kiely-Eng
Moody's Docutronics Information Services
195 Broadway, Suite 2004
New York, NY 10007
Tel: 212/233-7140; Fax:212/233-7173
E-mail: kielyenm@moodys.com

CHAPTER 6

DIGITAL LIBRARY CONSULTANT FOR A COMPUTER CORPORATION

RICHARD P. HULSER
IBM Corporation

INTRODUCTION

I am a digital library consultant for higher education at IBM Corporation, with responsibilities and focus on digital library opportunities and technology strategy planning. I began my professional library career as assistant librarian and then library director at Snow College in Ephraim, Utah. After returning to graduate school, my career continued as senior librarian at the IBM East Fishkill facility in New York. A few years later I began work with the marketing division of IBM in New York City. This was a non-traditional role. There I did consulting with libraries and museums regarding their planning and use of technology for information management. This role expanded over time to include higher education institutions nationwide and then on a global basis.

I received a BS in Earth & Space Sciences from the State University of New York at Stony Brook, a MEd in instructional media and instructional product development from Utah State University, and an MA in librarianship & information management from the University of Denver. I am active in many professional organizations, particularly Special Libraries Association.

How I came into my current job responsibilities is probably not totally unlike others now in non-traditional jobs. I suppose I always had an interest in information management. I remember often visiting the public library to get materials for school assignments or fun reading while growing up in Whitestone, New York. I thought it would be great fun to be able to work in such a place. Although I applied several times, there were many more baby boomers than jobs in the 1960s, and I never was able to get one at my local library.

My entry into the library workforce finally came about in my second year as an undergraduate student at S.U.N.Y. at Stony Brook. I was pursuing my interests in astronomy and earth science at the time and worked in the library to pay expenses while attending school. I had the good fortune to have excellent supervisors while working in the Earth & Space Sciences Library over the next three years. This proved to be a solid foundation for what was to become my future profession.

My interest in museums and science education gave me the necessary background to learn about alternative methods of education and information retrieval. This was done at the American Museum of Natural History, New York City, as part of an independent study project. I worked as a volunteer with school children and the visually impaired who visited the various exhibits, particularly the halls of dinosaurs and minerals.

I learned some traditional methods of search and retrieval while working at a probate court and archives in New York City. I worked for a company supplying a variety of services to law firms in the area. This required spending a great deal of time at the courthouses retrieving information and was my brief introductionto the legal information arena.

My financial circumstances at the time required a delay in attending graduate school, so I spent a year as a ballroom dance instructor. This experience, combined with my involvement with some college and community theater productions over the next few years, introduced me to the ongoing complexities of documentation and information transfer of the performing arts. It also helped me earn money as an evening instructor while attending graduate school at Utah State University. During this time I also worked in the curriculum library at the university and assisted with the first national conference on videodisc technology. It was here that I realized that local and national library meetings were important to my continued education and professional growth.

My dance background turned out to be useful in supporting the dance and theater arts programs among my duties at Snow College in Utah. This was my first professional library job. This job was a great training ground as we had a small staff and therefore did a variety of jobs in the library. A few years later I decided to pursue an additional graduate degree at the University of Denver and had a variety of jobs and experiences during that time. My library experience and science background enabled me to get a temporary job on a database project for a Denver oil company. This job required me to work as part of a team.

Teamwork was also important while a University of Denver graduate intern with the IBM library in Boulder, Colorado. That library experience introduced me to the information management needs and operations of the corporate world. I acquired a variety of skills working with other interns and the regular library staff, as well as maintaining my professional contacts as I continued my formal education. This experience led to a senior librarian position in the IBM East Fishkill facility in New York. Our library services supported product research, development, and manufacturing at the site. I also was project manager for a retrospective conversion of the card catalog and conducted database searches. This later turned out to be my last traditional library job.

An opportunity to work with the marketing division of IBM arose that enabled me to broaden my experience. I had already been working on enhancing my technical and marketing information retrieval skills, so this opportunity was timely indeed. The variety of my previous experiences enabled me to move into a non-traditional position as a library specialist for IBM marketing teams in the New York City area. It had challenges that required flexibility and a willingness to learn new skills. Marketing training, including honing of interpersonal skills and detailed education on products, were key components of my on-the-job education. While giving presentations was part of my previous experiences, this new position afforded many opportunities to meet with a variety of people to review information in many kinds of settings.

It was in this job that I learned first-hand about corporate restructuring and a new meaning to the word flexibility. The increased variety of work enabled me to demonstrate my skills and set the stage for increased responsibility as part of a team to support library needs for our higher education marketing teams nationwide. This work included participation in many presentations and demonstrations at internal and external national conferences.

Opportunities to work with clients as a consultant became a large part of my job and developed into a focus on technology strategy management. This also provided a base for a new area of work with our research and product groups who were developing digital library products and applications.

NATURE OF THE WORK

My responsibilities now focus on working with higher education clients and IBM client teams in North America to identify appropriate areas for the implementation of IBM Digital Library products and services. This often involves working with clients to determine how digital library applications can enhance their current and future information services. Part of my responsibilities involve presenting trends in information management to executives. This provides an opportunity to broaden their understanding of the library profession and our changing role in their organizations.

Much of my work involves teaming with clients and co-workers for a variety of time periods. This often requires traveling to their locations. I also give presentations about digital library projects and other topics at conferences and meetings throughout the year. As a designated "mobile worker" I am assigned a laptop computer for use in conducting business at remote locations, including my home office. I also have a mail slot and a telephone number at the local IBM office. I can go to that office to connect into the company network or I can dial into the network from a remote location.

Since I spend most of my time at client locations or in my home office, I have many challenges for information access and retrieval. My information access and retrieval requirements are a bit different from someone who works in a specific location all the time. I have to rely heavily on electronic access and delivery of information to augment regular mail and faxes. I need to be able to have access to information in a variety of formats, including multimedia presentations developed by others. Some of these are stored on my laptop computer, while others are accessed online.

Due to time zone differences or the lack of time I have to actually retrieve information, my need for information is often well beyond "normal" business hours. Thus, I am in a good position to understand the needs of my clients when discussing remote access to information services and management of these services. I am more of a user of information services than a provider, due to the nature of my work. Time and workload constraints also require that I rely on our corporate information services to conduct database searches and find information for me instead of doing such things myself.

Some of my work includes coordination with global clients and IBM colleagues as well. This sometimes requires traveling to their locations to conduct consulting sessions. This has built an addedappreciation of different cultures, an ability to manage work to interlock with people in various global time zones, and a broader perspective on global information management services.

POINTERS FOR ACHIEVING SUCCESS

There are a variety of skills and experiences that contribute to being successful in a non-traditional role. Flexibility and a willingness to gain new skills or explore new areas of responsibility are at the top of the list. The workplace is now a consistently dynamic environment where lack of change is the exception. There is ample opportunity to experience new things.

One of the challenges is to identify how to best utilize traditional information management skills to succeed in such an environment. I often use my library skills in

gathering details of a marketplace, assessing competition, or even gaining more knowledge about my company. My experience enables me to use our corporate information services more effectively.

Good interpersonal skills and presentation capabilities are qualities that are useful in any job, but they are essential to work I do today. An ability to work as a team player or to lead a team has been increasingly important over the last few years. It is not unusual for me to work as a member of many different teams over a short period of time, depending upon the need. A valuable skill is understanding your role on a particular team and maintaining that role throughout a project, as appropriate. Having an ability to deal with a variety of situations and people can make the difference between a positive and a painful experience.

Working in non-traditional capacities can be rewarding, but also challenging. It is sometimes more difficult to explain the value of your expertise. Measurements of success may include ties to revenue attainment and profitability. While having the opportunity to travel to many places and meet many people can be exciting, it keeps you away from home, family, and local friends. At the same time, it's great fun to meet friends and colleagues and share experiences more than just once a year. My travel opportunities require initiative to understand and appreciate cultures different from my own in order to be successful working with national and international colleagues and clients.

My professional association involvement provides an important and consistent link to colleagues and provides an avenue for ongoing education. My knowledge of currently available products and services, as well as trends and directions in the industry, are important since I work with librarians on a regular basis. I get this knowledge from conferences and meetings. It is always a struggle to keep up with such information, so it has to become part of your regular routine.

It can sometimes be a challenge to match association activities to ongoing work responsibilities. It may be difficult to justify to management participation in some professional activities if the job is very different from traditional library work. Keep this in mind when exploring alternative career opportunities.

My varied work experience and other background contributes to myability to continue to work in a non-traditional library role. I would venture to say that such work will become the "traditional" role of the future. Combining these provides an opportunity for a challenging and interesting career.

Richard P. Hulser
IBM Corporation
702 Quinnipac Ave. Unit B
New Haven, CT 06513-4007
Tel: 203/466/3155; Fax: 203/466-3155
E-mail: rhulser@vnet.ibm.com; Also: rphulser@aol.com

CHAPTER 7

INFORMATION OFFICER AT A LARGE ECONOMIC DEVELOPMENT BANK

SUSAN O'NEILL JOHNSON
The World Bank

INTRODUCTION

I attended library school at Pittsburgh in the 1960s. I was a medical faculty wife with small children. My idea was to get involved in a medical library environment where I would find flexibility in hours and in job types available that were geographically transferable. We moved to Kentucky, where I worked part time in the University of Kentucky libraries, set up library services and some automated reference services for a large medical research program, worked in reference at the public library, and was a leader in the local Friends of the Library group.

I became concerned about the state of the public library situation and image in the community, and started their Public Relations Office. In this role I helped department heads initiate needed but unfunded programs, started a newsletter, created a logo, held art shows, demos and benefits, hosted famous speakers and concerts, brought people into branches, and helped centralize an image of one library.

During these years I also obtained a real estate broker's license and a life insurance agent's license, and worked in these fields. I learned a great deal about the profit motives of people, and what drives them. As a broker you have to provide value-added services, or you will be dropped, and definitely not paid!

I decided to come to the center of all libraries, Washington, DC, and become involved in library automation. I was able to land a temporary job at the Library of Congress in 1984; then worked as the Audiovisual Librarian at Dahlgren Medical Library, Georgetown University; then for the IIT Research Institute in the Clearinghouse for Ada programming language information for the Department of Defense; and then as head of the Information Center at Jane's Information Group. In these progressively better-paid positions I learned as much as I could from students, colleagues, patrons, and all the training made available to me. My particular emphasis was on developing my computer skills and knowledge about information technology (IT) as it relates to finding and delivering electronic information to clients. Jane's downsized, and I had success in finding a job advertised by the World Bank at the SLA Job Bank during their annual conference in New York, 1989. I was just finishing a Masters Degree in Public Administration at American University at the time.

NATURE OF THE WORK

I have worked for the World Bank, the world's largest economic development institution, for seven years. It is a highly professional and stimulating environment, with an extremely well-educated and dedicated international staff. I was hired as the Information Technology, Facilities and Personnel Librarian, to manage one of the World Bank and International Monetary Fund's fifteen libraries. My clientele was anyone in either institution who was developing skills in desktop computing, or seeking knowledge in the vast array of IT topics, such as telecommunications, hardware, software, and portable computing. Excellent equipment had been put on all desktops, but without a great deal of IT support or explanation.

My department, in charge of computing infrastructure in the Bank, had been very aggressive in developing an enterprise-wide network. There was also another whole department delivering IT training. However, because of the decentralized structure of the Bank, the speed of IT change, and the necessary focus of my department on rolling out systems, a vast need developed for a reliable source of internal information on IT.

I renamed the library the Resource Center, and began emphasizing non-traditional ways people could find information about IT. I developed several user groups to get people talking to each other and to my department's experts. The user groups generated a high level of information exchange, demos, and informal communications for hundreds of staff. The most active clients were awarded "Honorary Friend of the Library" certificates at an annual celebration. A library newsletter turned into a departmental newsletter on IT, then it became the Bankwide newsletter on IT.

I realized this role of education through building information networks was becoming much more important to me than the traditional roles of book and periodical collections and reference. I took a serious look at what my goals really were, meeting the needs of the users for internal IT information, and concluded they could be better accomplished outside of the library setting.

The Bank was also in the midst of business process reengineering (BPR). One of the areas of success in BPR was in developing concepts that could potentially work in the Bank in IT customer support. For a year a group of people had studied how to improve the IT support since it was so fragmented, ineffective, and constantly under attack. It was determined that a new IS Support Center Group would be created in the IT department. Its primary focus was to eventually unite into one knowledgebase and one automated call distribution (ACD) system for all the IT questions in the Bank and its 76 resident missions. Its goal would be to take all the IT hotlines, help desks, and individuals providing institutional service on institutional standard products and databases, and virtually work together, reporting data into one system. The results would be better analysis of data, which could determine, for example, where training or more IT support staff were needed. I decided I wanted to join this Group.

Nature of My Non-Traditional Work

With permission from my manager, with whom I wanted to ensure a continuing relationship, I wrote a job description, and moved the user group and newsletter functions with me into the new IS Support Center Group. I now help the new Group promote and market the new support system, as it is developing. I learned its functionality firsthand by spending some time directly on the help desk. I also help promote other new services through the Business Technology Solutions User Group, which I had started seven years earlier. Different program series build awareness, for example, on a huge Lotus Notes rollout across the Bank, a little-understood document imaging system of internal Bank project documents with enormous potential, and portable computing issues within a networked environment. I am also setting up training using internal resources to combat computer viruses, largely coming in on diskettes from staff traveling in third world countries. I collect feedback from attendees and service users, then let the providers know about it, with some analysis and corrective suggestions of my own. I also continue to lead the Internet User Group, where speakers from all over the Bank discuss content, searching, intranet functionality, and standards.

The impact of my move has been very positive for several reasons. In my role as editor of the Bankwide IT Newsletter we are looking at the issue of reducing paper through use of pdf formats, and print previews using postscript printers. We expect our work to have Bankwide impact. I am also head of the department's Greening Initiative, in which I am at the forefront of technology changes that will preserve resources at the Bank while also supporting the business process. I now head a departmental committee of 25 interested staff, and we are writing position papers, then presenting them for discussion and management approval. Next we will design an implementation schedule to change the way people use computer resources (computers, printers, faxes). That is just the beginning, as we are also participating in efforts to change other behaviors including recycling and the use of public transportation.

With the Newsletter and user groups I still promote library services, invite and set up their participation to give programs on the Bank's intranet, on the web-based online library system, on how to search the Library of Congress, and on how to take advantage of a FirstSearch pilot, for example.

I have been active in a department-wide initiative to improve the skills of IT personnel, broadening their perspectives beyond their own specialties. Document management people, engineers, computer specialists, and librarians all need to know more about each others' work and think more about the business needs of the institution. I have brought in outside speakers for these purposes.

I also send business to my former Resource Center, and find opportunities to integrate them into the department. Where users gather, I point out the Resource Center that has the materials they need for follow up. I have facilitated bringing the Resource Center into an intranet project where they select an electronic full text reading list, and I work with a computer specialist who sets up the actual links to the licensed resources.

POINTERS FOR ACHIEVING SUCCESS

1. I recommend being active in organizations such as SLA and ASIS because of the opportunity to learn from other members. Being active in their programs, if my own experience is any example, could range from creating scholarship funds to producing musical satires at the World Bank to raise scholarship money. It's a lot of fun and often leads into fruitful professional relationships.I have found that giving papers at conferences is also a way to make one's projects more widely known.

2. Circulate among clients. Do not get a desk job where people have to come to you; meet them on their own territory.

3. Don't let bureaucratic barriers stop you from helping clients. While keeping your manager informed, start new initiatives.

4. Be loyal to your management and make them look good while making sure they know your efforts.

5. Don't let lack of resources slow you down. There are people resources surrounding you, just waiting to be asked to participate in something to make their work more meaningful. Find these people and create working relationships with them. You can meet over e-mail.

6. Have lunch with clients and colleagues, and create new ways to share information in an informal and non-threatening atmosphere.

7. Build loyalty, trust, and contacts.

8. Keep your sense of humor, listen to other people, and organize opportunities for you to act on good ideas together.

9. Help build reputations of your best supporters through communications and opportunities for exposure.

10. Find where the areas of need are in your organization and build up value-added services to meet these needs.

11. Learn to cut less-valued services.

12. Achieve as high a technical level as possible. You have to be a user to get energized about what is possible through IT, to create ideas and stimulate others.

13. Read, practice, and go to as many free or inexpensive sessions as possible.

14. Try to get tuition benefits from employers.

Susan O'Neill Johnson
The World Bank
R 6037
1818 H St. NW
Washington, DC 20433
Tel: 202/458-2833; Fax: 202/676-1270
E-mail: Sjohnson3@worldbank.org

CHAPTER 8

MANAGER OF INFORMATION RESOURCES AT A COMMUNICATIONS FIRM

DONNA SEES
Nortel, Inc.

INTRODUCTION

During my senior year of college, working toward a major in English, I was faced with that age-old question, "what do you do with a degree in English?" I took a research methods class, an advanced class for English majors. It consisted of researching various topics and finding answers to obscure questions. All the work involved spending many hours a week in the library. We were not allowed to ask the librarians for assistance. That research methods class is responsible for my career today.

My first library job was as the acquisitions assistant in a medical school library. My desk was in the Learning Resource Center (LRC) so, besides acquisitions, I also supported the video equipment and computers that were in the LRC. After one year, I became the administrative assistant; reporting to the assistant director of the library. Of course, I didn't give up all of the acquisitions duties. I added the responsibilities of tracking library expenditures and budgets, checking and compiling staff time sheets, writing minutes of all professional staff and support staff meetings, and acting as the backup to the OPAC operator. From this position, I saw all that was involved in running a library, and I decided that I wanted to have the assistant director's job some day. I went off to library school at the University of Michigan with the intention of finding a job in a medical library upon graduation.

The University of Michigan has an exceptional experience for budding librarians. The university residence halls have libraries. The residence hall libraries are run by library school graduate students. I was a residence hall librarian during my time at Michigan. The job is to run the library, including all the duties from hiring, training, and supervising staff, to collection development and budget responsibilities. It was a position that provided some experience in every aspect of library work.

After graduation, I worked in a public county library in the Adult Continuing Education (ACE) section. Information in ACE included everything from college information to how to conduct a job search. ACE also happened to be the computer center in the library, although the newest computer was about five years old. I enjoyed the work because of the people. It truly was a rewarding position. Many folks would stop in to let us know that they got a job or were accepted to school.

NATURE OF THE WORK

Life in a Corporate Library

Although I enjoyed the people in the public library, I knew that I wanted to work somewhere that technology and computers were more prominent. During a job fair at the University of North Carolina, I discovered an information specialist position at BNR in Research Triangle Park (RTP), North Carolina. BNR, now Nortel, is the research and development arm of Northern Telecom, a telecommunications equipment company. I was concerned that my lack of telecommunications knowledge worked against me but I soon discovered that it was the breadth of my library experience, particularly my residence hall experience, that worked in my favor.

I was one of four information specialists in the Information Resource Center (IRC) at BNR. We shared responsibilities for online searching, reference, and collection development. It took me about two years to become comfortable researching the industry, technology, and markets. I joined the library during the end of a growth stage. Several months after I started, budgets became an issue, and we entered two years of no growth. This had negative implications for advancement too. There was one library and one library manager. Thus, there would be a long wait before any of us ever got an opportunity to manage the library. As it happened, the Information Specialists were heavily involved with most of the budgetary and operational planning of the IRC. We created a wish list of new products/ services that we wanted to offer, new equipment that we wanted to purchase, etc. Each year we would do our best to put a new product or service in place that we thought we could gain support for or that we thought our budget would be able to support.

It was during this time that Nortel developed company documentation on CD-ROM, a product called Helmsman. The documentation folks approached the IRC to help get the word out about Helmsman. It was a great opportunity as we housed a large print collection of company documentation. For a time, we maintained both the print collection and a stand alone Macintosh with CD-ROM capability to run Helmsman.

Helmsman provided opportunities for me that changed my career path once again. I created a "Lunchtime Learning" session to train people how to use Helmsman. This was a one-hour session during lunch that covered the basic documentation structure and basic use of retrieving needed documents from the CD-ROM. Our engineers thought Helmsman was a great improvement over the paper version, but they wanted networked access so that they could look up documentation from their own desktops.

This networked access to Helmsman was the technical challenge that I craved. My first discovery was that the best way to network CDs is to literally load the contents of the CD onto a hard drive rather than run information directly from the CDs. Equipped with the Information System's technician's knowledge about response time from a server vs. CD-ROMs, I was able to solicit support for the purchase of a server to support Helmsman.

Networking Helmsman involved a variety of tasks and skills. My greatest learning came from the Information Systems group. I found a couple of great technicians who were willing to teach me about network traffic and servers. Once we had the server in place, training once again became the most important factor. I offered sessions monthly as well as individual sessions upon request. From the training sessions, more ideas were generated on how to improve the product. My database searching skills came in handy as I collaborated with the documentation group to improve Helmsman's functionality. Once we had the system up and running smoothly, I turned training responsibilities over to other IRC staff members. The Helmsman development folks continued to enhance the product, and they released a much-awaited UNIX version.

My next challenge was to launch Helmsman in a networked UNIX environment. UNIX was something that was completely foreign to me. We didn't even have a workstation in the IRC, so I had to borrow the use of a workstation to become familiar with the environment and then learn Helmsman in the UNIX environment. Again, I had to gain support for funding a UNIX server to support the product. Throughout my experience with this one product launch, I gained valuable technical knowledge that led to many more projects.

Soon, I was beta testing industry-specific CD-ROM products and traditional library CD-ROM products. On one occasion, our site was the sole site to actually get a beta product successfully networked. The product unfortunately was never offered commercially. I still receive calls from engineers who want to access that now defunct product. Overall, this was how we managed to bring new products on board during years with no budget growth.

After I had been with the company for three years, we had several staff changes in the IRC. Two of the information specialists left. Suddenly, I was the sole information specialist at my site as we had opened a branch site where the only other information specialist was located. My responsibilities grew to include supervision of the reference desk and our co-op students. Nortel's co-op program allows us to hire graduate students from the library school for up to three terms. We have two co-op students: one reference co-op and an information systems co-op.

A year after the information specialists left our group, our manager decided to take an opportunity in the Training Department. One of the former information specialists returned to our group to take the management position. This meant that I had missed a rare opportunity to move into management. I expressed my disappointment to the new manager. She was about to go on maternity leave in a few months, and I asked to act as manager during her leave. This was the first time that I asked for an assignment specifically with my future career in mind.

After our manager returned, I was promoted to senior information specialist. Basically, I became responsible for the day-to-day operation of the IRC. The staff had become accustomed to asking me for decisions and advice from my stint as acting manager. It allowed our manager to do more planning functions. Her main goal was to move our group outside of the "administrative support" groups that reported to finance and into an organization that valued our services and was more closely aligned with the company's bottom line. She targeted an organization that had most of our heavy users. This group was part of the Systems Engineering Division responsible for long range and strategic planning among other functions.

A special telecommuting project was starting up at about this time. A group of people at our site wanted to show that telecommuting was possible for our company and our customers.They put forth a business plan that would support a small group of forty people from a cross section of groups to telecommute. I submitted my name for the pilot and was selected. I began working three days a week at home. Since I was part of the pilot project, there was no formal technical support. This project, therefore, added to my own technical knowledge and skills as I had to troubleshoot my own problems at home.

At this time, my position was largely traditional with the exception of the technical projects that I continued to work on. I expressed interest in becoming more involved with systems work. Our IRC database was becoming an albatross as we continually needed more powerful functionality. There were many bugs that required fixing. After a year as senior information specialist, we created the system specialist position. I was to find a solution to our database problems as well as support and develop our IRC systems.

We successfully moved from the "administrative support" group into the Systems Engineering Group. As a result of moving into their group, the IRC gained many opportunities to participate in projects across the Systems Engineering organization. First, there was a special project that had seed funding from two vice presidents. This project was to take a look at how the division came up with new ideas and developed them for product design. The goal was to reengineer this process for faster time to market.

The IRC manager was attending a regular staff meeting when she heard about this project and suggested that I should become involved. They needed research at the beginning that I could provide. Also, they had talked about creating a database as one aspect of this project. I was identified as a possible consultant in the database design. One reason for this role was the fact that I had also participated in another group that was looking at futuring exercises as a way to do strategic planning. It seemed to be a good mix of skills to work as a team member on this project.

After my successful involvement with this special project, I was asked to lead a team in evaluating and redesigning the arrangement of the lab's quality documentation. The IRC's parent organization was responsible for coordinating the ISO and other quality initiatives for the lab. My skills in networking documentation with servers and my information organization skills were perfect for the project.

There was another group that was working with systems thinking, which was a way of analyzing processes and problems by considering the big picture—the whole system or end-to-end process. The IRC manager thought that this might be a useful tool for the IRC to analyze its processes for reengineering. I was assigned to the project with the systems-thinking person. We worked together to design a model of the IRC and all of its functions. It took three weeks of intensive work, but it identified those areas that needed reengineering in order to free resources. As a direct result of the systems-thinking IRC model, I was offered my non-traditional position, manager of Customer Service Programs.

The IRC at RTP is one of nine libraries within the corporation worldwide. A high-level management decision was made to consolidate the libraries into one management reporting stream. Up to this time, we supported our specific site and reported to local management. Now, the Information Resource Network (IRN) supports the entire company regardless of employee location and reports to one common director. As part of this reorganization, a position was identified for metrics creation and tracking and user needs analysis. The position also involves supporting the IRN with process design and documentation. Another tremendous responsibility of this position is to create a call center for IRN customers to call. The call center is a phone number for all IRN customers to call, regardless of location, to reach the IRN. One might think of it as a virtual reference desk. This call center is still in development, but we have the great knowledge of a telecommunications company to help us through this process. Along with the call center, we are designing a database to support the IRN work. This will allow us to track our workload and resource deployment. It will identify who our customers are and what their needs are. As Customer Service Programs manager, it is my responsibility to write the specifications for the database. Another group within the IRN, Global Information Access and Networking Tools, is designing the database.

The database will make metrics tracking easier as it will automate the process. Currently, we categorize questions received into three categories: inquiry, in-depth inquiry, and research. These, for now, are the common metrics tracked across the IRN. Some sites still track legacy metrics such as article requests, ILLs, etc. My job is to introduce standard measurements for these services across the IRN.

Currently, everything is tracked on paper. The database will change this process to be less time consuming. We will also be able to report metrics in a variety of ways that would be prohibitive using our current process. There are many processes yet to be worked through and documented.

The IRN is a year old at this writing. It's been a busy year of working through processes and responsibilities. We are mandated to serve the entire corporation worldwide, and we hope that our call center as well as our web pages will help us to be successful. We are also planning to open a library in Asia. Once again, I took control of my career and volunteered for the Asia assignment. I will be in Hong Kong for six to nine months. My new title and position will be a traditional one again, manager, Asia/Pacific Region, Information Resource Network. I consider it just one more step in a long journey. It will be interesting to see if I continue along the traditional path or venture out to new territory upon my return.

POINTERS FOR ACHIEVING SUCCESS

My job required a bachelor's degree with an MLS at the time I was hired. It still would today, but I would recommend some MBA courses or experience for my current position. I learned on the job over the years and have worked closely on projects with MBA graduates, which gave me an opportunity to learn from them. A database structures course was very helpful to me. A statistics course would definitely help too.

The most important skill that I've gained over the years is networking; the ability to identify people who can answer my questions and teach me what I need to know. In today's changing environment, it's impossible to know everything. The best thing a person can do is acknowledge a shortcoming and find someone to help change that weakness into a strength.

Corporate environments are constantly changing. The maturity of the corporation will have an impact on the work environment. There is a corporate life cycle that will influence how the job is going from one year to another. It is critical to learn to adapt. Change can also be seen as an advantage from the standpoint that change often leads to opportunities. This type of environment is best suited to someone who is willing to take risks and try new things.

It is important to focus on new products and processes and to continue to look for opportunities for further growth and development.

Donna Sees
Information Resource Network
Nortel, Inc.
35 Davis Drive
Research Triangle Park, NC 27709
Tel: 919/991-7925; Fax: 919/991-7909
E-mail: dsees@nortel.ca

CHAPTER 9

PROGRAM DIRECTOR FOR A NONPROFIT CONSULTING FIRM

CYNTHIA W. SHOCKLEY
Logistics Management Institute

INTRODUCTION

As the only woman director in an non-profit consulting firm that works in a highly political environment, surrounded by retired military officers and senior executive service individuals, I continually find that people are surprised that my graduate degree is in library science (whenever that happens to come into a discussion). I always tell them that my training is not just in working with books and that I have skills beyond that of what is considered a typical librarian. I look forward to the day, if it ever comes about, when we aren't limited by the outgrown concepts about the capabilities of library-trained people.

Why did I pick librarianship? It all started during my childhood. Growing up in a small town on the Eastern Shore of Maryland I read voraciously, always filling up my summer reading club list. I discovered early how much I loved the children's section of our library, which at the time was housed in a rambling nineteenth century home. Some of my neighbors were librarians who were world travelers and went to places I could only dream about.

When I began my undergraduate program at The George Washington University, I needed a job to supplement my various sources of income. On a lark I called the Smithsonian Institution's employment office, was put on hold, and when someone finally came back on the line they asked me what I wanted. I said I was a student and interested in part-time work. The person replied, "Oh! Well I just got off the phone with a scientist who is looking for a part-time student assistant. Are you interested?" I think I set a land speed record to that interview and for the next three years diligently pursued tracking down citations and their full publications in the field of invertebrate pathology. Then I began the tedious task of creating a database using paper tape (now I'm dating myself!), which was then converted to magnetic tape and put up as one of many National Cancer Institute databases. A budding information scientist was born!

After trying unsuccessfully to get into law school (a blessing in hindsight!) when I graduated, I found that with my experience at the Smithsonian I quickly found a job as an information specialist working for the General Electric Corporation at the National Clearinghouse for Alcohol Information. From there a consulting firm hired me to help design a new government clearinghouse - the National Clearinghouse on Aging Information. This project was my first taste of consulting, and I found that I had an aptitude for such endeavors. I worked for a couple of small consulting firms in the Washington, DC area over the next several years and then had the fortune of crossing paths with Jerry Kidd, a member of the faculty at the College of Library and Information Services (CLIS) at the University of Maryland. Dr. Kidd convinced me that I should pursue a masters degree in library science.

After some initial resistance, I went through three years of night school and emerged with an MLS degree. Attending CLIS opened up new doors of opportunity for me and introduced me to individuals who were doing significant consulting in the field. While completing that degree, I worked with Davis (Dave) McCarn, who has turned out to be a long-term friend and mentor. Dave had just retired from the National Library of Medicine and was asked by The H.W. Wilson Company to chart their path from hot lead to electronic publishing. I was Dave's "horse holder" and worked as his assistant in crafting the requirements for what is now known as Wilsonline. From associating with Dave I was able to hone my consulting skills and learned that it is acceptable to say to a client, "I do not know the answer to your question, but I will find out."

Through Dave I was introduced to Don King of King Research. Again I was further exposed to the world of consulting in library and information science and assisted on projects for the National Science Foundation and NASA.

All during this phase I was getting more exposure to the world of computers and automation. I remember the intense excitement Dave McCarn and I had logging onto the British Library at 600 cps using a Cromemco Three microcomputer (this being 1980) with a script carefully orchestrated to respond to a whole series of questions and passwords!

Although I was not proficient in programming, I found that with my newly acquired background in library science, I could envision how the pieces of an information system needed to come together as a successful blend of database record design, classification and indexing, and facilitated user interfaces. I realized how important standards were a concept not part of my thinking prior to my MLS studies.

Information systems that are created without regard to standards that can apply to them, find that they cannot integrate with larger domains. Although I never will be a cataloger, the premier importance of thinking about how to classify, index, and catalog "records" or "data" so that they will become useful information to some user sometime in the future, is a lesson carefully learned in library school (and one I can thank Dr. Hans Wellisch for) and applied to most of my consulting work ever since.

The next leap in the combined worlds of librarianship, automation, and consulting found me as the beta site manager for the Integrated Library System undergoing installation at the Pentagon Library. The system was being modified from the version created at Lister Hill. Because of this two-year endeavor, I found a niche area of consulting that continues to this day for me, i.e., interfacing between end users and system developers and programmers. Like the reference interview, as the liaison or "interpreter," you must hear the concerns and questions of the user (or patron) and appropriately interpret them. A good consultant has the same skills as a good reference librarian - you must listen carefully and ask probing questions in order to provide the most meaningful answer. If I didn't thoroughly understand the error or problem that the users identified as a result of testing the software, the programmers would embark on the wrong solution. Since this was an integrated package, an incorrect programming fix would produce other problems elsewhere in the system—if not immediately, then at some later point in the testing. Incorrect fixes would start to produce an endless round of chasing the problem, and the system would never be right!

To try out my skills as a librarian, I accepted the position of assistant director of the National Epilepsy Library and Resource Center at the Epilepsy Foundation of America. Although I loved this job because I felt that I was contributing to an enriched information environment for people with epilepsy and their families, I found that I chafed at participating in day-to-day operational duties. I kept identifying opportunities for the Resource Center to be an internal consultant to other departments as well as extending its automation reach to other associated communities in government and academia. The lesson learned here for me was that I do not thrive in an operational environment. The field of consulting with its cycles of identifying, participating in, and completing project after project for a variety of clients has more appeal for me. This was and has been my only attempt at being a "real librarian."

Consulting

Learning this lesson at the Epilepsy Foundation convinced me to make a serious inroad into the world of consulting. I accepted a position with Price Waterhouse; not as a librarian, but as a senior consultant in their Law Firm Services Group, a specialty consulting practice. My job (again) became one of interpreter, i.e., working with large law firms in the United States and Canada to identify their automation requirements and convert them into solid requests for proposals. In addition to a fast-paced existence on the road—my clients were primarily in Atlanta, Toronto, and Chicago—I was also exposed to a structured project management environment. Price Waterhouse sends its newest staff members to consulting "school," and the firm requires annual attendance at workshops designed to polish and augment your skills. I was promoted to manager and continued to sharpen my abilities to "multi-task" by handling several projects in different cities with different clients.

Much as I enjoyed consulting, I found life on the road too exhausting, and decided to accept a position with a Bethesda, Maryland-based nonprofit consulting firm. The shift from the dizzying pace of "Big Eight" consulting to a slower, more academically oriented situation with Logistics Management Institute (LMI) was wonderful. I found a more appropriate blend of the change of pace that comes with turnover of consulting projects with schedules that better permitted more reasoned automation strategies for clients and less pressure to identify new work in order to move on to the next client. In other words, I could think through what the requirements for a client were and how to create an automation strategy for them without having to jump on a plane for the next city! As a research fellow at LMI, I had consulting opportunities that led me to author such reports as "The Defense Technical Information Center (DTIC): Meeting the Scientific and Technical Information Challenge of the Future," "User Requirements Analysis for the NASA Intelligent Gateway," and, "Functional Description of the NATO Scientific and Technical Information Service."

Striking Out on My Own

After six years at LMI, and armed with a good background in how to work with clients to best determine what they should and could be doing with automation, I decided to strike out on my own. In 1992 I founded my own consulting firm, Information Resources-Information Strategies, Inc. or IR-IS, Inc. This was a difficult decision and one that left me wondering if I had abandoned security for a whimsical departure into self-employment. This phase of my career, which lasted four years, taught me how important networking can be to the survival of a newly-created consulting practice. In a way, founding my own consulting firm returned me closer to my librarianship roots since I wanted to consult with other librarians, but there were several lessons still to be learned.

Although clients were willing to pay significant sums of money for an hour of my time while employed by Price Waterhouse or LMI, this willingness did not translate when I became IR-IS, Inc. Lesson one: name recognition is invaluable. My main marketing targets were other librarians who required assistance in developing automation strategy plans and then determining how to execute those plans. Lesson two: typically librarians are not funding decision makers. This lesson required me to learn to be more patient and to make more convincing arguments to upper management about the role of the library to the entire enterprise.

During these four years I also developed a working concept of what I call the "unified field theory of information" (apologies to the physicists). As part of my networking activities, I belonged to several professional associations, namely ASIS, SLA, ARMA, and AIIM. What intrigued me was that each group was essentially trying to view and solve the same problem, i.e., how to manage a segment of information (whether internal or external to the organization). Information was information was information, whether MARC records of monographs or engineering drawings or images of internally published reports or data acquired from a weather satellite. Eventually I envision a merger of these various disciplines—librarianship, information science, records management, documents management, data management, etc.—into one that works with information as a totality.

NATURE OF THE WORK

For some inexplicable reasons, LMI recently invited me to return to head up their Information Management Group, and now I find that my career has turned from active hands-on consulting to one of managing resources, i.e., people, equipment, projects, and budgets. LMI was established in 1961 at the recommendation of the Secretary of Defense as a nonprofit organization to improve business management at the Department of Defense. I am one of twelve program directors. I head up the Information Management Group, and have a staff of twenty who have a broad range of expertise in information technology.

My primary responsibility is to make sure that these twenty people are happy doing what they're doing (their skills span a wide breadth of experience from senior information resource management strategists in their sixties to younger technologists whose consumption and mastery of software tools is mind boggling), that enough new projects are coming in the door to continue to keep them industrious, and that everyone feels taken care of, i.e., the computers, software, and other necessities are up to their requirements. My management style is, as defined by one of my staff, "walking the shop floor." I see each person in the group every day. I also meet regularly with all our clients, identify new business opportunities, prepare proposals, manage the group's budget, and attend a lot of meetings! The energy output is tremendous as I try to guide our group into new opportunities without making anyone nervous!

POINTERS FOR ACHIEVING SUCCESS

Most people who meet me in my current position assume I have an educational background in business or computer science. Those skills acquired in a graduate program would be helpful, but much of what I do requires good common sense integrated with the ability to get people to work together in teams. Sensing what makes someone feel fulfilled in their work and determining ways to let them head toward that goal is essential. Understanding the nuance of technology at this time, for me, has taken a back seat. Having good project management skills, i.e., getting to the conclusion of a project with viable products and recommendations for the client within the allotted budget, are still very useful.

As for success in consulting, I should point out that consulting and stability are often not synonymous. Consulting as a career requires risk taking since your career and salary are not guaranteed when you accept the position. You have to continually redefine and augment knowledge and skills to keep up with clients. Or you will risk having those clients find other consultants who can keep up with the technology. The pros for me have always been a challenging environment that requires me to continue to read voraciously, ask a lot of questions, and think about how we need to make technology productively work for us. I have never been bored!

Cynthia Shockley
Logistics Management Institute
2000 Corporate Ridge
McLean, VA 22102-7805
Tel: 703/917-7554; Fax: 703/917-7468
E-mail: cshockle@lmi.org

CHAPTER 10

SYSTEMS DESIGNER AND CONSULTANT

GAIL THORNBURG
Consultant, OCLC Online Computer Library Center, Inc.

INTRODUCTION

I am one of an increasing number of persons equipped with library and information science [LIS] training, who has moved into non-library work. I received an MLS from Kent State, then went on to complete a Ph.D. in Library and Information Science at the University of Illinois in 1987. The master's degree I viewed as providing a set of skills to help me find things. By the time I reached Illinois, I knew I wanted to look at philosophy of science as a means of understanding the structure of information. I wound up getting involved with related issues in artificial intelligence, implementing an expert system using multiple experts-- reference librarians in the sciences--to explore knowledge representation in pre-query search formulation.

When I finished my doctorate, I went on to become an assistant professor at the University of Maryland. There I taught the bibliographic organization of knowledge, library automation, plus a doctoral seminar in knowledge representation. At this point, you might say I had a standard script for one type of LIS career. It featured rules such as, do good research and publish in the right journals, teach as well as possible but not at the expense of research, serve on committees, and give talks or do other forms of public service--the usual set of rules and relationships that an assistant professor [aspiring to tenure] uses as guidelines for organizing his/her work. For a librarian working in, say, a large public library, the script would have held different facts and inferences and would have assigned different priorities—but most would agree on the existence of a career model.

NATURE OF THE WORK

Departure from the Standard Script

Because of my marriage, I wound up resigning from Maryland and moving again. This led me to look at work outside traditional library schools. My script for an assistant professor was useless here, so I did some exploring. I did some independent short-term consulting and proposal development, and took the time for a course in C. All the while I was developing new contacts, learning new skills, and half-subconsciously gathering the raw material for a new script. I found my first long-term consulting position working on an ISDN implementation project at NCR. None of my co-workers quite understood what I did, but I was having fun. (Rule one for my new script.) This project sparked my interest in networking. I worked at NCR for a year, followed by other consulting projects in information management for a litigation support database, and various other efforts.

Next I spent a year working at Fox Software, especially in indexing and authority control issues, but also other publishing work. There I learned about the intense climate of a software company working hard to meet a deadline for a new product release—many nights and many weekends. But by the time I left, I had noticed the elegance of the Foxpro DBMS environment, and resolved to find a way to work with it more.

I had my chance to do so when Frontier Engineering called. My first project with Frontier involved a feasibility study on porting a small FoxBase DBMS application to a Sun UNIX platform. Unsure just what would constitute feasibility, I went ahead and tried getting it to work for a start. The report I figured out later; the staff writers euthanized all my "best" flights of phrasing.

Electronic Publishing and Groupware

Once I'd finished this project, someone wondered aloud if I'd happen to be interested in the Request For Proposal (RFP) & Source Selection Project at Wright Patterson Air Force Base. Was I! This intrigued me from the point of view of electronic publishing, and the promise of further database work, as well as learning Windows development. (I liked staying close to the code.) Because I'd worked, prior to getting my MLS, as a government contract negotiator, I recognized the importance and high visibility of the prototype. I wasn't afraid to work in a pressure environment with difficult clients, and this meant an opportunity to be involved in one of the most interesting projects Frontier had to offer.

I was project leader on this prototype for over four years. By the time I left, we had not only developed the means for publishing complete RFPs, potentially thousands of pages, but had seen them deployed in other locations. Considering diverse publishing tools, we wound up using highly customized Word templates, with lots of code behind the scenes. This had the advantage of grass roots appeal—government users across the country could take our templates and add code to customize them further, without the need for high-priced publishing software. I also had the responsibility for a CD server offering virtual library access to government specifications and standards, available on a LAN and inter-LAN basis. This was the first such networked CD server environment on the entire base. We had a bulletin board service set up with dial-in and Internet access for sharing draft RFPs. There were database tools to support our users, such as one I developed in Foxpro to convert data from proprietary format databases into one multi-merged "flat database" suitable for mail merging into editable Word forms. That was one popular little program.

In my last couple of years there, we decided to start developing software for source selection teams using Lotus Notes. Source selections are as "closed" as RFPs are "open". Requirements for security of a contractor's proposal information is absolutely critical, and there's usually a lot of money at stake. We needed tools that provided security "out of the box." We needed to be a client-server database environment to handle the multiple changing sources of information. And we needed as rich a set of programming tools as possible, since our development staff was quite limited at this point. Lotus Notes was the vehicle of choice. And so I became intensively involved in software development in that most arcane and unfriendly version 3 of Lotus Notes.

In addition, this involvement opened the door for me to pursue my interest in networking. Hey, someone had to get those servers talking to each other! I fought to get the essential training, and studied nights to become certified as a Lotus Notes administrator. Having done this, I wound up in charge of a multiplatform, multidomain Notes server environment running on OS/2, Windows NT, and OS/2 SMP. Along with this came all the network responsibilities, setting up an SMTP gateway, Novell administration tasks, etc., that I could possibly desire. I set up a firewall for our teams, to allow the conduct of electronic commerce. The server room where I worked had the flavor of a situation comedy, with a procession of users entering stage left, exiting stage right —spiked at times with server crashes, enterprise network problems, and the occasional brainstorming design session. And I had marvelous coworkers. The hours were long and pressure was intense, but the experience was one of a kind.

So great, that some of my teammates had difficulty understanding why I would leave that environment to go to a project where I'd be working in a totally dissimilar environment, on an IBM mainframe at that. The project, however, was not really a prototype anymore. And if it's not a prototype, I asked myself, why am I here? The project I'd heard about at OCLC appeared to offer the prospect for interesting information problems, potential use of my AI background, and perhaps more research and publishing down the road. It seemed only logical to go for it. While it meant turning my back on a very marketable Lotus Notes certification, I figured that LIS professionalism is more than any one specialized tool competency. That might not be a rule in everyone's script—especially when tool competencies seem to command so much respect and pay so well.

POINTERS FOR ACHIEVING SUCCESS

What have I learned from all this? Value your teammates. Nothing is more important than a good team for the success of a project. Don't count on publishing ALL your most interesting work—some companies have strict secrecy requirements due to market competition. Expect to work hard, count it as a privilege to work long hours if you're learning new skills, and expect to need to learn new languages or network skills all the time.

Interestingly, despite my technical skills, the last three jobs I've taken were purportedly because of my LIS background. I don't say I would have had the offers without the technical skills.

Expect to work at times alone in a sea of information infidels. A great project team will often feature no other persons with LIS degrees. For me, professional society involvement has lent a certain balance in these situations. Writing papers about my work, making time for outside research, and giving presentations has also been helpful. And taking the time to read LIS journals that aren't directly work related? Sooner or later, how many areas are not related to the management of information? Little is wasted.

Don't let that intensive involvement with specialized knowledge acquisition blind you to the need to take a higher level view. The need for regular abstraction from one's daily tasks is no luxury, just as sufficient levels of abstraction should be a workplace criterion for anyone with a script like mine.

Sure, it's important to be authoritative in one's areas of responsibility. That was the immediate effect of my studying for Notes certification: better answers for my users. Helping users, I've learned, can be a very real source of satisfaction. Especially when you have the wherewithal to be of real help!   So many careers are changing fast in this post-industrial society, people everywhere are striving daily to regroup. This is a chance to be so mutually reinforcing! Build your own schema for your ideal work, but don't leave out the satisfaction of helping others build theirs.

Gail Thornburg
Consultant, OCLC Online Computer Library Center,Inc.
Database Quality Group   MC 246, Kilgour Bldg.
6565 Frantz Rd.
Dublin, OH 43017-3395
Telephone: 614/761-5246; Fax: 614/798-5742
E-mail: thornbug@oclc.org or thorn@fsp.fsp.com

CHAPTER 11

MANAGER OF CONTENT LICENSING FOR AN INTERNET-BASED AUTOMATED RESEARCH SERVICE

SARAH WARNER
Amulet, Inc.

INTRODUCTION

Little did I know that when I began my professional library career in the tradition of Dewey and Ranganathan that many years later I would use my cataloging skills in the hottest new company to hit the online information industry. I received a BA from Adelphi University and an MLS from Pratt Institute. I started out as an assistant serials cataloger responsible for cataloging of engineering and computer-related English and foreign language serials at the Engineering Societies Library (ESL) in New York City. After several years in cataloging, I joined the ESL reference staff as a research librarian working with professional engineers who were looking for information in such fields as civil, environmental, mechanical, and electrical information. I later joined Parson Brinckerhoff Quade and Douglas, a major international architectural/engineering consulting firm as library manager. Again my focus was on international engineering, architecture, and some business information sources. Two years later, I joined Wang Laboratories as corporate librarian, where I expanded my knowledge of engineering, computers, and business information research sources. In addition I worked closely with the computer industry analyst community to provide competitive intelligence information.

In all three libraries, I was required to know where to acquire and locate the answers to customer inquires quickly. At Wang the information research tools included a collection of over 300 specialty computer and engineering titles. Among these titles were all the IEEE and ACM titles. The collection also included product and company data on CD/ROM such as Disclosure, Computer Select, and UMI PROQUEST.

I spent many hours defining search strategies, learning new search techniques, and executing searches using Knight-Ridder's Dialog Information Service. Knowledge of the premium content providers such as the Yankee Group, Forrester Group, and other content providers such as Information Access Corporation and Ziff Davis were essential to respond to our library customer's inquiries.

I saw first-hand at Wang the results of the downsizing and budget cutting of the library/information center. It was a natural progression with the growth of the Internet that information requirements would shift. This was particularly evident in research and development, where the engineers were the first to insist on having the information on the desktop by being the savvy Internet users.

NATURE OF THE WORK

I then moved to Amulet Inc., where I became manager of content licensing for this Internet-based automated research service company. I have made the leap from a traditional library and information center environment to a leading edge entrepreneurial climate among the new early adopters of the push/pull information-based environment, where time is measured in Internet years, which is only several months. My primary responsibility is to research, identify, evaluate, recommend, and license new content for their InfoWizard service. In addition I work closely with the InfoWizard product engineering design team to integrate the content into the InfoWizard service. I am responsible for tracking the implementation of the licensing contracts.

Amulet particularly sought me out for my expertise as a professional searcher and my knowledge of high-technology information sources. Also, my extensive experience in both cataloging and reference have been invaluable in the fast-paced environment of the Internet. There are others with a masters in library science on our team, who perform other critical functions. It is this same understanding of the breadth and depth of information content sources and experience working with the computer industry consultants that I have transferred to my work at Amulet. My understanding of the sometimes arcane and costly research retrieval process has been very valuable when working hand-in-hand with the Amulet engineers to correctly automate the research process. Amulet's first service offering, InfoWizard, focuses on Information Technology. Amulet licenses and redistributes content from periodical publishers, business news providers, newsletters, and business publishers and redistributes a comprehensive mix of branded and distinctive content. Amulet has licensed content from authoritative sources, all of which were very critical to research at Wang. These sources include CMP Media, COMTEX, CorpTech, Computer Review, Faulkner Information Services, Information Access Company, Information Sources, International Computer Programs, Lycos, Inc., Newsbytes News Network, PR NewsWire, and Reuters.

Amulet's InfoWizard is a revolutionary, Internet-based automated research service. InfoWizard is the first agent-based personal research service designed for people who evaluate, buy, market, sell, or support information technology products and services. InfoWizard provides reports at a very low cost that help business professionals make better informed decisions concerning technology topics. It also helps them identify new business opportunities while keeping a close watch on customers and competitors. My previous experience has been invaluable as we bring this service to market.

I am responsible for day-to-day direction. There has been a major shift in the daily assignments and the degree of responsibility and direct involvement in projects. At Amulet, there is both the opportunity and the requirement to participate and be actively involved directly with the development of the InfoWizard service. This is contrasted with many years at Wang, where the library customers drove the transactional activities. The biggest change is that, for the most part, I drive my activities of the day. At Amulet, for example, my primary responsibility is to match our customer information needs with available online information sources. In a typical week, I can be investigating prospective new information sources and the content for possible licensing, analyzing, and synthesizing the information, and discussing my findings with others on the team. The valuable skills that I have honed over the years come into play. I research a variety of information sources by using the traditional research techniques, talking to my professional colleagues about what content sources they use, and, of course, focusing many hours on the Internet.

This research has involved locating both information on a specialized content and on the provider. In addition to understanding the content, it is also important to understand the publisher or aggregator's competitive strengths and weaknesses. Researching the various content providers in information technology and general business is the first step in what can be a long process from research, analysis of the sources, and the inclusion of the source in the InfoWizard service.

In parallel, once it is determined that there is a possible match, I call the sources to discuss the possibility of licensing their content for the InfoWizard service. This is where I go into a selling mode in order to convey the message that joining with Amulet is a win/win situation. I market and sell the opportunity that Amulet can offer the information content provider a new opportunity to broaden its distribution channels and expand its customer base by getting in on the ground floor. The next phase that I am intimately involved with is related to a variety of activities associated with preparing the licensing agreement and negotiating a deal. This includes analysis of both the business and legal license agreement terms that almost always include a series of discussion with our outside counsel.

Closing the licensing agreement is just the beginning. In a typical week there are various activities in my role as liaison between the content providers' technical contacts and our engineering team. As part of the contract management activity there are discussions related to the data speeds and feeds and distribution methods and how to incorporate the new content into the InfoWizard Service as it related to the terms of the license agreement. As part of the content team, I also have been involved in testing of the InfoWizard service and have worked with the team to design the template query forms and the classification of information in report request template sections to meet the customer's needs.

For the most part at Wang, I was most involved in the operation of the library; however, with drastic downsizing, I juggled both the administrative tasks and reference and research. The daily reference/research responsibilities were transactional in nature, and in most cases the library staff never found out the end of the story--whether the information had been useful or not. The ready reference assignment or reference project to a greater degree, would allow limited involvement with a particular project. The interaction with the information requester or an intermediary would be very intense for a relatively short time period, but the very nature of providing reference services often prohibits one's ability to see the conclusion of a project. Over the years there were a few select projects that I was involved with including extensive company research for various merger and acquisition activities. I also wrote and communicated competitive information to product development, marketing, and sales teams in the field when I packaged and distributed custom research for the Competitive Intelligence Report Service.

It is thrilling and exciting to be part of an Internet start-up company and to have an opportunity to participate in a vast variety of activities from building an information service to bringing it to the marketplace. It was a tremendous moment for all of us when our first customer submitted a credit card for an InfoWizard report.

POINTERS FOR ACHIEVING SUCCESS

There are just a few watch words that I would like to leave you with regarding how to think about your career.

1. Reach out to your customers.

2. Continue to publicize your library programs along with non-traditional ones.

3. Be willing to change your priorities.

4. Be willing to take risks.

5. Roll up your sleeves and do what is required to get the job done (this is the most important word of advice I can give you).

Sarah Warner
Amulet, Inc.
360 Mass Ave.
Acton, MA 01720
Tel: 508/264-0333 x113
Fax: 508/264-0909
E-mail: swarner@amulet.com

CHAPTER 12

INFORMATION SPECIALIST IN AN ENVIRONMENTAL CONSULTING FIRM

LARA J. WIGGERT
Environmental Management Support, Inc.

INTRODUCTION

When I made the decision to earn my master's in Library and Information Science, I had just left my second position as a research assistant in a biomedical laboratory. I was one of those individuals with many interests who was having a difficult time deciding on a career path. After earning a BS in Biology and completing two years of graduate work in Nutrition and Food Science, I changed my mind about wanting to pursue research on a professional level. As dissatisfying as the research was for me, however lab work seemed to be my best option for employment at the time, given my educational background.

When I learned that my younger sister had decided to pursue a library science degree, my options seemed to open up. Here was a chance to combine my love of books and learning with my interest and training in the natural sciences. Why hadn't it occurred to me before? I'd never given much thought to what kind of education and training was required for professional librarianship, and no one had ever suggested it to me as an option. I realized my experience must have been all too common after I began my master's program in Library and Information Science at The Catholic University of America in January 1992. I discovered that I was one of only a handful of students in the program with a science background, which ultimately worked to my advantage. There are many sci-tech libraries around the country, and most seem to prefer or require education or experience in the sci-tech realm.

NATURE OF THE WORK

Shortly after I began library school, I obtained a graduate assistantship at the USDA National Agricultural Library's (NAL) Biotechnology

Information Center. There I gained invaluable experience providing reference and referral services to a diverse clientele made up of government and business representatives, academics, students, and members of the general public. I also developed and performed numerous online searches of NAL's AGRICOLA database to produce published bibliographies on a variety of biotechnology topics. In addition, I was responsible for collection development, vertical file maintenance, and training new graduate assistants. My science education served me well as I set about learning the language and concepts of agricultural biotechnology. That knowledge base enhanced my ability to design effective database search strategies and provide coherent, useful information in response to individual client needs. As part of my library science degree, I completed the Special Libraries Association's management course and two online database searching courses in preparation for a full-time professional position in a special library.

After receiving my MSLS, I took a reference librarian position with INFOTERRA, part of the United Nations Environment Programme information network, located in the U.S. EPA Headquarters Library in Washington, D.C. This was another sci-tech information center contained within a large library, similar to my situation at NAL, so the transition was fairly easy to make. My position was newly-created, with the primary responsibility of providing technical information to participants in an international pollution prevention project. I performed many online database searches in order to identify relevant EPA documents and put together topical bibliographies, and prepared customized information packets tailored to each client's needs. I welcomed the opportunity to establish my own small collection and define a modus operandi for my successor to follow.

My experience at EPA helped me obtain my current position as information specialist with a small environmental consulting firm. We support several offices within the EPA, and much of our work involves either using or producing official EPA publications, so my understanding of the agency's document system and organizational structure has been valuable. As with my previous positions, both my science background and library science training serve me well here. In general, each staff member has a particular area of expertise, but our work is not necessarily defined or limited by our degrees.

My work is interesting, varied, and definitely non-traditional. I maintain a small, uncataloged reference collection, but our company does not have a library. My clientele consists of my fellow staff members and our EPA clients. Everyone, including myself, manages multiple work assignments, and is responsible for writing a work plan, developing a budget, and tracking work progress for each project. Although specific to libraries, what I gleaned from my Special Libraries management course helped me in this area of planning and budgeting. I regularly search technical, business, and news databases as well as the Internet, and manage document delivery in support of various research projects.

My responsibilities include producing a bi-weekly technical information report on innovative hazardous waste remediation technologies. This involves maintaining alerts in multiple databases, reviewing search results for relevance, editing, reformatting and organizing records into pre-defined categories, and formatting a final document. One of my first projects was a comprehensive bibliography of EPA publications on innovative remediation technologies. Working on this document required me to learn how to use a graphics program, so I now have yet another new skill at my disposal! Recently, I produced a report on North American sites available for testing these types of technologies. This involved developing a questionnaire for each site, making appropriate contacts, and subsequently summarizing and organizing the information into a coherent document, which will soon be released as a new EPA publication.

I am proud to be the primary author and designer of an official government document, and no doubt will be asked to do more in future. Another area of responsibility for our company is provision of meeting support. One aspect of this involves attending conferences to take notes, and then writing up the minutes. I enjoy doing this from time to time for the opportunity to travel to interesting places, and because I like to write and am confident in my ability to comprehend technical discussions and report on them effectively. My library science training in information organization helps me in this endeavor, I believe.

Overall, I am pleased to have found a position in which I can take advantage of my science background and utilize my skills in obtaining, interpreting, and organizing information in ways different from the traditional librarian. I confess I have never enjoyed cataloging, for instance, and, though I recognize it as a valuable skill, prefer not to have to do it. I also appreciate the varied nature of my work. I am rarely bored, almost always busy, and I never know exactly what I will be called upon to do next. Being a non-traditional "librarian" has its advantages!

POINTERS FOR ACHIEVING SUCCESS

For anyone interested in a non-traditional sci-tech librarian/information specialist position, I think it is most important to be open-minded and flexible about the kind of work you might be asked to do. If you are the type of person who prefers a pre-defined job description with few surprises down the road, a non-traditional position may not be for you.

On the other hand, if you enjoy variety in your daily routine, and are eager to learn new skills and discover new ways to apply your librarianship training and experience, as well as utilize any sci-tech education you may have, such a position may be just what you're looking for.

I would also recommend reviewing any sci-tech education/training you may have received. This may mean getting back in touch with some of your old text books or notes, or perhaps adding several good references to your collection geared toward your topical area of work. For example, I have a comprehensive dictionary of scientific and technical terms, as well as several chemistry and environmental engineering texts that I refer to often.

Lara J. Wiggert
Environmental Management Support, Inc.
8601 Georgia Ave., Suite 500
Silver Spring, MD 20910
Tel: 301/589-5318; Fax: 301/589-8487
E-mail: lwiggert@emsus.com

Part Two
Entrepreneurs

CHAPTER 13

INFORMATION SYSTEMS CONSULTING FOR AN INTERNATIONAL CLIENTELE

RON DAVIES
President of Bibliomatics Inc.

INTRODUCTION

I am a library and information systems consultant. I have been effectively self-employed since 1987, most of that time working under the aegis of Bibliomatics Inc., the company I founded, and of which I am president. Bibliomatics has no full-time employees, but undertakes work on larger projects in cooperation with other consulting companies or by engaging associates for the duration of the projects. The work itself covers a wide range of services, including developing systems-related information strategies; needs assessment and requirements analysis; system design, implementation and integration; and programming. While in the early years of the company, this usually involved library-related systems, increasingly these systems are more broadly based full text or Internet-based retrieval systems.

My education is not atypical of the people now in their mid-forties or older who work in textual information systems, in the sense that it involves as much informal as formal education. My undergraduate degree was in Linguistics from the University of Toronto; while I had done some programming in high school in Toronto (not at all typical in the late 1960s!), the Computer Science program at that university in the early 1970s was heavily mathematical, and certainly at the time held little interest for people who might be interested in textual information retrieval. After graduation, I spent five years in theatre management before returning to graduate school and getting a Master of Library Science degree from the University of Western Ontario in 1980. My intention in going to library school had been to become a reference librarian with subject specialization, but a librarian mentor had pointed me to the Western program as more technologically advanced than the other schools in Canada at the time. The graduate course work re-awakened my interest in computer systems. I took all the systems-related courses I could, and when they ran out, undertook an independent study project under the supervision of Prof. Jean Tague comparing bibliographic and database software that resulted in a published paper.

NATURE OF THE WORK

When I graduated, I had two job offers, one as an indexer and the other as an acquisitions librarian in a Canadian university library. I choose the second, in part because the university library was planning on acquiring an automated acquisitions system. The process of examining in detail several acquisitions systems allowed me to continue with practical study of library and information systems. As an employee of the university, I was also eligible to take undergraduate courses free of charge, so I took several courses in computer architecture, application development, and assembly language programming. In addition to managing a search and orders section with seventeen employees, I spent lunch hours in lectures, and evenings (often until the wee small hours of the morning) studying and doing course assignments. It was grueling, but very worthwhile.

After almost two years at the academic library, I was hired as a library systems analyst at the International Development Research Centre (IDRC), a small Canadian aid agency that supported research into the problems of developing countries. IDRC was very highly respected in the information field for their sponsorship of library development and information dissemination projects throughout the world, as well as for MINISIS, an information retrieval software developed by IDRC in the late 1980s. I spent three years as systems analyst with the IDRC Library (which used the MINISIS software) designing databases, managing systems, advising on procedures, and designing a performance measurement system. My work also involved some collection development and user liaison, which has been extremely useful to me in my work since then in understanding the needs of library users. I was also involved in activities beyond the narrow confines of my job description, most notably in giving two, three-week software training courses in Indonesia and Korea. After three years with the Library, I moved full-time to the MINISIS support and marketing group, at first writing computer documentation, and later as the person responsible for software support, training and distribution in Africa and the Middle East. In many senses I was already working as a consultant, helping organizations in these regions to implement information retrieval applications, advising on language-related issues (i.e. the use of Arabic), training users and liaising with locally-hired trainers in some regions. After three years with the MINISIS group, I left IDRC and began to work as an independent consultant.

Because of contacts made originally through my work at IDRC, my clients have mainly been international organizations, though I also have a fair number of Canadian and American clients. I have often remarked that consulting practices tend to focus on one type of organization. If, in your professional career, you have always worked with public libraries, it's likely that you will find it harder to attract academic or special libraries as clients. Whether it's fair or not, clients tend to feel more comfortable with consultants who have demonstrated experience with similar types of organizations as well as similar types of services.

Success in library and information systems consulting requires basic computer knowledge and skills. These are much easier to acquire now than fifteen or twenty years ago. When I first started with IDRC, the organization was in the process of acquiring a 512K memory upgrade to their main minicomputer for over a thousand dollars! Affordable microcomputer software has also put computing power within the range of everyone, a far cry from the days when I had to get up at 4 am on a Sunday morning in order to get time on one of the university's single-user DEC minicomputers. The increasing popularity of document management, records management, and, of course, the Internet, means that there is now tremendous interest in the problems of retrieving information. Subsequently, a variety of courses that deal with retrieval or that discuss retrieval problems in a more general context are offered at universities or technical colleges. While there are many people of my generation who are in important EDP, MIS, or software development positions with undergraduate degrees in economics, English, even classics, I think today an undergraduate minor in computer science or at least a strong selection of university or college-level computer courses is an essential requirement.

More important than this basic computer literacy is a willingness and interest in continuing to learn. Computer hardware, software, and application environments change almost completely every five to seven years, and you must be willing to spend a lot of time outside working hours reading, experimenting, and learning. Finding time for this continuing education is not easy when you have a full-time job, but when you are running a consulting company, and you don't get paid unless you are doing billable work for a client, it is even harder. In my own case, new software products, the obsolescence of old software, increasing interest in full text retrieval, the rise of new languages such as C++ and Java, and of course the rapid development of the Internet as a means of delivering information services, have completely changed the nature of my consulting business. While basic computer knowledge of machine architectures, languages, and databases is an essential starting point, it won't get you very far unless you are willing to invest a lot of time and effort in learning.

POINTERS FOR ACHIEVING SUCCESS

You need to be familiar with a wide variety of information retrieval systems from a practical as well as theoretical perspective. I still think this is best obtained through a masters degree in library and information science, information science or information management or one of the computer science programs with strong emphasis on information retrieval. Regardless of the name of the program, it is important to get exposure to a wide variety of retrieval systems and to focus on general principles, not on the specifics of individual systems, catalog codes, or standards. To give an example, I work with MARC-based information systems, but I also work with many systems that are not based on MARC, AACR2, or other traditional library standards. In some cases, it makes sense to use MARC. In other cases, it is not necessary, and you need to keep an open mind and know that you can still provide high quality information services using other standards.

There are other technical skills that are very important in managing a consulting practice. The ability to write quickly, clearly, and easily is a real asset. I have always enjoyed putting pen to paper—or rather fingers to keyboard—and it is no drudgery for me to do so. If you are advising a client on a management strategy, you need to be able to write a succinct, clear, and convincing report in a very short period at the end of your consultancy. Your report may be the only concrete product the client receives for the money you have been paid. So no matter how much thought and research you have put into arriving at your conclusions, if the report reads poorly, the client will feel cheated. If you have developed an information system or application for a client, it is also essential to document your work. In part, this is so that the client can understand and maintain it, but it's also for yourself: a year (and ten projects) later you are not going to remember the details of your implementation without documentation to prod your memory. If you can write well and quickly, you can provide documentation at a minimal, and highly competitive, cost. Technically talented people who cannot write will struggle in a consulting practice unless they hire someone who can do the documentation for them.

A consultant is someone who has specific skills and expertise, but a consultant is also a businessperson. More important than any of the technical skills a consultant brings to a project are the business and people skills. First of all, you need to have a strong set of basic business skills. Your skills don't have to be sophisticated. I couldn't explain to you the fine print on my corporation's year-end financial statements, but I do understand basic accounting practices and know enough budgeting to be able to draw up a budget. I can plan for (and have the discipline to manage) cash flow. I know how to draft terms of references and contracts. And I don't have difficulty in controlling expenses (when expenses have to be checked) and or in spending money (when it's important to the future of my business to do so). My work experience before entering library school was all project-related, and one of the great assets I acquired almost unconsciously from that experience was the ability to manage projects and to plan for and (more importantly) meet deadlines. While initially I did not have to market my services, since clients tend to come to me through recommendations of former clients, it is a skill that I am continuing to learn and develop.

You must have the ability to relate well to people. One problem full-time employees with permanent positions face is the ability to get along with co-workers whom they may see day in and day out for years at a stretch. The consultant has a different problem, working closely on a project with a dozen or more people whom he or she may never have met before. You don't need to win any popularity contests, but you do need to be able to relate well to people, to size up their strengths and weaknesses without prejudice, to deal honestly and openly with people at all levels of an organization, and to inspire in people a sense of your own competency and trustworthiness. This may sound difficult, but it can also be a tremendous lot of fun. The opportunity to get to know people from different backgrounds in a variety of different walks of life working for organizations in a dozen countries, has been a very satisfying aspect of my career.

I also think that you need to be something of a perfectionist. You can't be so much of a perfectionist that you can't finish a project (or you will never make enough money to live on), but you must have the discipline to do an excellent job every time you go to work for a client. My personal goal is to ensure that, on any project I work on, no one I know could have done a better job. I can't emphasize this enough in terms of making a success of a consulting practice over more than a two-year period. Eighty percent of Bibliomatics' clients return to the company for futurework, and at least four or five clients have been hiring my company to do work for them on a regular basis for five or more years. Almost every new client that approaches me is doing so on the basis of work I have done for former clients, or on recommendations supplied by them.

Running a systems consulting business is not easy. Irregular and often long hours, extensive travel, and the continual responsibility of ensuring that the business side of a consulting practice is well managed can be difficult, particularly if you attempt to fit in family responsibilities. On the other hand, the opportunities to undertake challenging projects, to meet a variety of interesting people, and to use and develop new skills and knowledge is unparalleled. I wouldn't have missed the opportunities I have had for the world.

Ron Davies
Bibliomatics Inc.
48-200 Owl Dr.
Ottawa, Ont., Canada K1V 9P7
Tel: 613/523-7981: Fax: 613/523-4417
E-mail: rdavies@bibliomatics.com

CHAPTER 14

FROM FINANCIAL MANAGEMENT TO LIBRARY MANAGEMENT

GLORIA DINERMAN
President, The Library Co-Op, Inc.

INTRODUCTION

Until I was seventeen and went off to college, I lived in a rather dysfunctional household. There were a lot of adults all going in different directions and me. As the only child of an Earl Carrol chorus girl and a Marine recruiting sergeant, as the only niece of two highly motivated and professional aunts, as the only granddaughter of two grandparents who did their best to bring some normalcy into the chaos, I couldn't help but feel a little odd in a suburb of New York that was the prototype of conformity.

Independence came early, and once I got used to the fact that being like everyone else was an impossible turn of my psyche, I led a relatively happy existence with absolutely no plans for a career. Let the reader remember that marriage and babies were rather the norm in the olden days.

Brown University awarded me my undergraduate degree with majors in English (the writing discipline) and psychology, my own true love. Since I knew that to be employed in the field of psychology in any meaningful way would demand at least a master's degree and probably a doctorate, and having no burning desire to go through the rigors and disappointments of authorship, I took the first job that came along — working as a secretary for the vice president in charge of investments at a large New York Bank.

In 1969 I became employed as the director of training in a major brokerage house. I got there because I needed work and a friend of the family was a big producer and a member of the elite inner circle who makes policy and hires friends and relatives. There were, at that time, 62 people in the Wall Street Training Directors association, and I was the only woman. As one of the guys, I was accepted as long as I maintained a standard of training proficiency, didn't seek special recognition, and contributed to the activities of the organization. In spite of the commute from New Jersey to New York, I loved my job, wallowed around in the prestige, devoured the insight into finance, and was content, if not ecstatic, with my co-workers.

Then in 1974 the virulent ax descended, and I was downsized along with about 75% of my colleagues. So much for security and an excellent record of accomplishment. My mentor had died. 1975 brought me into the State of New Jersey as an investment advisor to municipalities and counties. A few years later, when I was looking for some divergent activity, I was invited to join the Board of Trustees of the library in my township. We were the second largest library system in the state, and I learned first-hand about the politics, the unions, civil service, work ethic, and what skills made a good reference librarian. I also learned about the problems, the salaries, the supervision, the vendors, and the quest for recognition. It was important to my director for me to become nationally active, and I served on the Board of the American Library Trustee Association for eight years. I was surprisingly comfortable in the library atmosphere and being apart of the policy making body. Then again, in 1980 I went through another downsizing, and that ended all predilection of working for anyone but myself.

From then on I stopped being a victim of management judgment and began to trust my intelligence, skills, drive, and imagination to become successfully happy and/or happily successful. If my talents could not be employed to serve me well, then, and only then, would I revert to a position where I had no control of my future.

NATURE OF THE WORK

After two experimental years of sweating through contract personnel work and professional recruitment, with consistent encouragement of my library director and several professional acquaintances, I decided to enroll for my MLS and start my own business. At the time, I wasn't quite sure how my company was going to be focused. It would begin with temporary help, of course, since that was the area that I knew best, but I was really interested in projects that would serve to enhance the importance of the library and librarians. My non-traditional mind-set was keeping me alert to trends, possibilities, reasons to expand beyond the reference desk, and onto the cutting edge of information innovation.

So there I was—trying to start an enterprise that my mother would be proud of, going to library school, substituting in school libraries, and doing library assistant work just to get experience and to learn the language. One of my first big breaks came from a major university, a massive shelf reading job that took twenty people ten days to complete, and it was during that project that I met someone who was very knowledgeable in automation. This was my first one-on-one experience with a computer guru. He loved to talk about the differences in the mega-systems that the university was struggling with back then. Every new concept opened a window of enlightenment, and I searched for reference sources that would broaden my understanding and explain the vocabulary. I could only follow about 10% of our discussions—well, they were not really discussions. He discoursed a monologue, and I added a few words of encouragement. But my business sense was in gear, and I multiplied his enthusiasm by the thousands of other universities in the country, and then added the seats of higher education in Europe and Asia, and I realized that traditional methods of library practice were fine but advanced technology was better—even though I wasn't very advanced as yet.

From November 1982 through December 1985, I worked from my home with two part-time assistants. I knew early on that to create a time effective environment, it would be smart business to have the clerical necessities done for me and to concentrate my energies on getting business and recruiting candidates to perform the contracts. Many people who start their own business get bogged down in the detail of opening the mail and paying bills. I got my secretarial help from our local high school business majors, and they were delighted to have the work experience. I also trained them in the manner that I expected the work to be accomplished, and left no procedure or routine to be innovated by a student.

In 1986 we moved into my office condo, complete with sign on the door, an umbrella stand, and a mortgage I was relatively sure that I could cover as long as I didn't take a lot of salary. What makes our scope of services so inclusive and so effective is the fact that I won't and don't say "no" to anything. If there is no one on my immediate staff who can address a new challenge, then I find an expert outside of our company who would be willing to review the salient points of the inquiry and comment on the feasibility of taking on the assignment. Knowing where to look is essential to my type of operation—reference librarian in search of an obscure fact.

If the job description of a traditional librarian is defined as a professional who is skilled in a specific area of work, such as information specialist or technical services associate, and is not expected to become proficient in divergent skills, then none of us at Library Co-op is traditional. My business goal developed as an amorphous structure—to form a company that could do anything that any library or information center needed when it did not have the time or personnel to accomplish the extra work.

Some of the more unusual services that we perform regularly are automation consulting; database development and customization; vendors of INMAGIC and CASPR software; construction and evaluation of user surveys; consultanting for records management; space planning; moving and shifting of library collections; and my favorite—library development when we are given an assignment to start a library where none now exists. We have implemented projects for the handicapped, the poor, and the extremely wealthy. Sometimes the lack of sophistication of our clients is staggering. Sometimes their brilliance is overwhelming.

Laird Consulting (Library and Information Resource Division)

Following the trend of the times, I started Laird Consulting about two years ago to work with accounts that exclusively needed our assistance with automation problems. If the time ever comes when we have to exchange our library business for another field, I want to prepare now, and that preparation has begun with name recognition. Although Laird is a division of The Library Co-Op, it has its own brochure, its own logo. Clients outside of the profession are more comfortable with the non-library designation.

My Outlook on My Company

I do a fair amount of speaking related to the profession and how I got started and what it takes to keep going seems to be of great interest. Guts and luck are mandatory, and you *cannot be afraid to fail*. If failure has a grip on your subconscious, it will dominate your business sense, and you will be tentative about making a decision. You will also be afraid to take a chance, and that's what business is all about--taking chances. The personality structure that belongs to a traditional librarian is not at all similar to the personality structure of a person who does well in business. Although both assist clients and are happiest when their efforts are acknowledged and appreciated, the person in business is proactive and therefore aggressive in developing a working relationship with clients that will be the foundation for an effective company. Motivated by money and spurred by success, recognition and satisfaction follow in lock step order. Promotion is key to getting the work; near perfection is key to earning repeat business.

The traditional librarian accommodates the needs of patrons because he/she is fulfilling the precepts of his chosen profession. Most of his decisions are reactive to the needs of the moment. Department planning follows the lead of management. When it is your business, you are management. The entrepreneur strives for satisfactory completion of project assignments because a happy customer is the best advertisement that you can buy.

Five reasons why the non-traditional path suits me well.

1. I like being my own boss. I'll never get fired.

2. I like the challenge of difficult decisions and if I make a mistake, then I'll take the blame and correct it.

3. I like the challenge of getting business.

4. I love working with the wonderful and diverse people who are part of my regular staff. (We're up to eight.)

5. I love to learn and every day is a learning day. No two days are alike—no two clients are alike, no two projects are alike.

Five reasons why I hate being in business for myself.

1. I hate haggling with the clients on the cost of a job.

2. I hate having to dun people for money after we've completed our work.

3. I hate potential clients who ask for a lengthy proposal and then give your ideas to a favorite son (or daughter). We are very careful about our responses to RFP's now.

4. I hate having to work holidays and weekends to get a job done because it was promised on a deadline.

5. I hate to fire people. This is sometimes necessary with contract employees who are not performing up to the standard we have set. It has never been necessary with any of our office people. As a matter of fact, in the fifteen years that we have been in business, we have only had four people who have had to be replaced, all for personal reasons or job advancement.

Have I been lucky?? You bet.

POINTERS FOR ACHIEVING SUCCESS

Six ways to create your own luck.

1. Be sensitive to your market — whatever it is.

2. Read every technical journal and professional publication that will affect your progress.

3. Get yourself known to the people who will hire you. Join the professional organizations and at least one service group such as the Chamber of Commerce.

4. Don't be afraid to toot your own horn. Go out and get the business — don't wait for it to come to you. Two of my best contacts came from seatmates on a plane.

5. Always carry business cards and give them out liberally.

6. Be enthusiastic about your company. Advertise. Where would Coke be without constant advertising?

Six things you should do before going into your own business.

1. Have enough money on hand to be able to carry your expenses for at least six months. Cash flow closes more businesses than lack of work.

2. Have the moral support of your family and/or friends. It gets very lonely.

3. Make sure you are strong enough to sacrifice time and recreation for your higher goal.

4. Invest in good office equipment and attractive stationery. Appearance counts.

5. Avoid nay sayers. Negative vibes have no place in your new venture.

6. Do what you like and like what you're doing. And when the time comes that it's no longer fun or satisfying—you can always write your memoirs!

Gloria Dinerman
The Library Co-Op, Inc.
3840 Park Ave., Suite 107
Edison, NJ 08820
Tel: 908/906-1777; Fax: 908/906-3562
E-mail: 71334.3036@compuserve.com

CHAPTER 15

METAMORPHOSIS OF A METALLURGIST INTO AN INFORMATION SCIENTIST AND ENTREPRENEUR

DONALD T. HAWKINS
President, InfoResources Corporation

INTRODUCTION

The library and information science field is very diverse, so there are many avenues by which it may be entered. Many of these paths involve courses and other formal training, often obtained at universities and library schools. In contrast to these fairly traditional training avenues, my training for working in the sci-tech information business was unusual: I did not have any formal library training! Although my entire 25-year professional career has been spent in the electronic information business, and therefore I have received much experience in information science, my formal training was as a chemist (with a BS degree) and a metallurgist (with MS and Ph.D. degrees from the University of California, Berkeley). I am often asked how a person with advanced technical training in chemicals, metals, and alloys came to be in the electronic information business. The quick and facetious answer is, "Through the back door!" The following account of the twists and turns of my career illustrates some of the significant developments in information technology, shows how much information professionals and their careers have changed, and provides some good lessons for those contemplating entering the information field.

Let us begin our tale in 1960 when, by a fortunate series of events, I found myself thrust into the world of graduate-level scientific research in the metallurgy department at the University of California, Berkeley. I became an undergraduate assistant to a professor and his graduate students. At that time, the state of the art in information storage and retrieval consisted mainly of manual techniques with some mechanical aids.

Database Creation

The project I joined involved compiling scientific data on metals and alloys, then critically correlating, analyzing, and disseminating the data. Considering that there were about 80 known metals and several hundred binary combinations among them, collecting data and information on these metals and their binary alloys entailed a significant effort, and, as one often finds, the information component of the project was critical to its success. At first we used edge-notched cards, which was a rather laborious process, with one card for each reference. I did not know it then, but the stack of cards formed a database, and watching the retrieval process quickly taught me the meaning of Boolean AND operations (although, of course, nobody told me that was what they were called)!

I soon learned the disadvantages of edge-notched card technology: it was slow, the cards got damaged and lost by use, and the amount of material became unmanageable. It became apparent that an alternative had to be found; several instances of major references being missed and the resulting embarrassment drove the point home. Fortunately, technology had been advancing, just as it does now, and a set of "optical coincidence cards" (commonly called "Termatrex cards" after their brand name) was obtained. I was commissioned to convert the database from edge-notched cards to the Termatrex technology, which worked on the principle of light passing through holes in cards representing subject terms when they contained the same document number. Using Termatrex cards, I not only learned about indexing and Boolean operations, but I also learned an important search principle; if the search was made too restrictive by using too many term cards, it might return fewer hits.

Bell Laboratories Corporate Information Retrieval Environment

After completing the requirements for a Ph.D. degree in metallurgy in 1971, I was extremely fortunate to join Bell Laboratories. At that time, the high-level information retrieval service of the Bell Laboratories Library Network was staffed by three information scientists. The job advertisement appeared in technical, not library, journals (I saw it in *Chemical and Engineering News*) and asked for candidates who were "familiar with technical information" and who also had an advanced degree in an appropriate technical subject. The Library Network management felt that if their information scientists had Ph.D. degrees, they would be perceived by the technical staff as fellow researchers. Thus, they would be better able to interact with them on an advanced level and would better understand the technical issues stimulating their information requests. This policy had proven to be very successful, but it has generally been abandoned in today's environment, not only because of the costs of hiring holders of advanced degrees, but also because it is unnecessary due to the profound advances in electronic information. The emergence of the Internet and World Wide Web have made it possible for virtually anyone to access information. (I hasten to add that it is not my belief that trained librarians have become superfluous because of the Internet; there will always be a need for professionals who know how to access and retrieve information and, most importantly, evaluate its quality.)

At Bell Laboratories, I joined two other information scientists who conducted literature searches and compiled bibliographies on demand for technical and management employees. I was able to apply my technical knowledge in information retrieval activities, but because of the breadth of technical interests of the Bell Laboratories research staff, I soon found myself involved in searches well removed from the subject of my training. My colleagues and I wrote the following in one of our earliest papers that described our experiences with online searching systems (1).

"It is interesting to note that while our Information Scientists have backgrounds in the physical sciences, they cannot control the information needs of their community, so sometimes one has the situation of physicists and metallurgists searching the business and psychology files for references on job enrichment."

The Library Network management also encouraged the information scientists to maintain their technical expertise by attending seminars sponsored by the research department that were of interest to them, and also to develop interests in related areas (both technical and library-oriented). Because of their advanced subject training, the information scientists were also assigned other special projects that arose from time to time. For example, I indexed some books, and one of my colleagues became a proficient computer programmer and developed a sophisticated machine indexing program that was widely used throughout the company, not only for bibliographies but also for internal company documents, directories of library resources, and even books. The third member of the staff developed an interest in managing library systems and is now employed by the Library of Congress.

Of course, technical subject training alone does not make a successful library professional. Recognizing this, the orientation program for the new information scientists at Bell Laboratories called for a series of visits to various support units of the Library Network. The program involved frequently providing traditional reference services on a backup basis, as well as a one week "internship" at the reference desk. Shorter visits to other support units of the Library Network, for example, cataloging, book purchasing, and technical reports, also provided valuable on-the-job training in library operations.

When online searching emerged in 1972, it was obvious that the information scientists should investigate and coordinate this new service. I immediately began learning about the databases and the technology of the systems, and my colleagues and I developed what became a full-fledged online information service operation. Because Bell Laboratories was one of the earliest commercial customers of the online services, we worked closely with the vendors, and I gained many valuable insights into the workings of the information industry.

I left the Library Network in 1986 and moved through a variety of information-related projects in AT&T's business units. One of these was an in-depth study of the electronic publishing industry (2) when it was in its formative years, and AT&T's management needed to learn about the industry and receive recommendations for potential new products. Because of my in-depth knowledge of the information industry and the very valuable contacts I had made in my early years, I was also the "content manager" on several product trials, including AT&T Network Notes and the AT&T RightPages service. (Neither of these services was ever deployed commercially because of the emergence of the Internet and the World Wide Web.)

One important phase of my career was attendance at and participation in technical conferences on information services. Professional meetings of this sort not only provided extremely valuable contacts but they also yielded much cross-fertilization, visibility, and idea stimulation for improving services related to my job.

NATURE OF THE WORK

After retiring from AT&T in June 1996, I formed an independent consulting venture, InfoResources Corporation, which offers services to database producers and other companies in the electronic information business. The major areas on which I consult are information sources and the use of the Internet for information retrieval, database marketing, and training. The experience I gained in promoting AT&T's Information Retrieval Service, using online systems, and performing searches as an intermediary for end users has given me an excellent foundation in the areas of training, database design, indexing, and the user interface. Because of my many years as a user of online services, I am able to bring that viewpoint to my consulting activities and thus have been involved in testing new products and services and in helping emerging companies in their product introductions. I have also worked on indexing projects and have consulted on the user interface to online systems.

Life as an entrepreneur is, of course, vastly different from life in the corporate environment. The most significant difference is that no support services are provided; the entrepreneur must do everything. In my case, what I miss most is access to an excellent technical library and all the associated services that were automatically provided. (For an "information junkie" like me, the change is not unlike undergoing withdrawal symptoms!) There is much available on the Internet, and public libraries are very helpful, but there is no substitute for a well provisioned technical library with access to the professional literature of one's field of interest.

Another difference between the entrepreneurial and the corporate environment is that an entrepreneur must do marketing, accounting, purchasing, and a myriad of other tasks that a person in a large company may take for granted. Such tasks are necessary, but they take a significant amount of time that cannot be used in income-producing activities. Of course, many features of being an entrepreneur are highly positive, especially the freedom to control one's own time and to do the things one enjoys.

During my career to date I have enjoyed writing papers (over 130 published), and becoming a two-time winner of the UMI/Data Courier Award for excellence in published online papers.

POINTERS FOR ACHIEVING SUCCESS

After a career spanning over two decades, one might expect that I have learned some lessons. Here are some of them.

1. Be alert to changing technology and exploit it. Technology will continue to impose changes on our world. Resisting them will only lead to failure.

2. Training and education, and especially experience gained on the job, are vitally important. In a changing environment, flexibility is necessary. One cannot be too restrictive in outlook, whether it is in conducting an online search (recall the lesson of the Termatrex cards!) or making a career decision.

3. Constant vigilance and readiness to adapt to change are required. Do not make the mistake of thinking you are indispensable. Apply your skills to changing situations.

4. The importance of professional activities, especially networking, cannot be stressed too highly. The best opportunities are generally discovered through networking.

5. With the emergence of the Internet and World Wide Web, the electronic information industry has entered a new phase. Today's environment is a far cry from that at the beginning of the industry, but it is no less interesting and exciting. I remain optimistic and enthusiastic about the future.

REFERENCES

1. Hawkins, Donald T.; Stevens, B.A.; and Pierce, A.R. Computer-aided information retrieval in a large industrial library. In: Lancaster, F. Wilfrid. ed. *The use of computers in literature searching and related reference activities in libraries*. Urbana, IL: University of Illinois; 1976: p. 31-55. (Proceedings of the 1975 Clinic on Library Applications of Data Processing)
2. Hawkins, Donald T.; Smith, Frank J.; Dietlein, Bruce C.; Joseph, Eugene J.; and Rindfuss, Robert D.; Forces shaping the electronic publishing industry of the 1990s. *Electronic Networking*. 2(4): 38-60; 1992 Winter.

Donald T. Hawkins
InfoResources Corporation
59 Twin Falls Road
Berkeley Heights, NJ 07922.
Telephone: 908/508-9777; Fax: 908/665-1649
E-mail: D.T.Hawkins@worldnet.att.net

CHAPTER 16

DEVELOPER OF KNOWLEDGE MANAGEMENT SYSTEMS

ANDREA MEYER
Founder of Working Knowledge

INTRODUCTION

In college, when I sat down to take one of those career interest tests, I was filled with trepidation. I knew that my favorite activity was writing research papers. I loved going to the library, digging around for all sorts of information, and putting together new ideas into a research paper. "But who's going to pay me to do that?" I told the career counsellor. "That's something you do as a student, not as a career."

But to my surprise, I learned that there was a whole field of study—library and information science—devoted to the topic of organizing and providing access to information. In particular, the profession of special librarianship focused on delivering information to a select group of users to meet their specific needs.

I was hooked. I enrolled in library school at the University of Texas at Austin and received a masters degree in library and information science. Because of my interest in special libraries, I wrote a thesis on the topic, which gave me a good understanding of what special libraries were and what they could potentially be. Specifically, I gained the insight that a library could be thought of as a service, not a place. That is, it wasn't just a physical storehouse of knowledge, but a process of delivering information to those who needed it. This insight intrigued me, and being able to describe the concept during a job interview landed me my first professional-level job.

In my job at the corporate library at IBM in Austin, Texas, I got a taste of various aspects of corporate librarianship. I provided reference service to engineers and scientists, (to support new product development) and to managers (mainly in the areas of competitive intelligence for acquisitions and training/psychology areas for employee development). I oversaw the circulation of books, assisted with collection development, and learned a lot from the library manager, Anita Lesser, about how to demonstrate the value of a corporate library to upper management.

But I also learned what I didn't like. My main job duty was online database searching. I enjoyed doing this when the topic was business or management, but cringed when the topic was engineering. I didn't have a background in engineering, and worse, I wasn't very interested in learning about it. I knew I'd never be very good at providing reference in this area because I wasn't intrinsically interested in it.

So, in 1986, I took a job with CareerTrack, Inc. CareerTrack is a company that presents one-day management training seminars across the country. The position I took with CareerTrack — to set up their corporate library — was exciting to me because the topic was completely business and because CareerTrack had no clear idea of what they wanted from a library. It was an opportunity to set the direction for the library and to introduce the concept of a library as not just a storehouse of materials for employees, but as a source of research to develop CareerTrack's training seminars.

Within three months, I was able to get the library to be a part of the program development department and to start providing research services to develop the seminars. Besides establishing the library, the projects that I did while at CareerTrack include the following.

1. Writing ten workbooks to accompany the seminars.

2. Research for CareerTracking, a book published by Simon & Schuster.

3. Writing two weekly and one monthly columns.

4. Co-authoring an audio-tape program, "How to Develop a Corporate Library."

How did I get to do all these projects? Quite simply, I volunteered. In some cases, my volunteering didn't meet with much response, like volunteering to write the workbooks. So I just wrote one and showed the completed project to my boss. Sometimes people don't think you can do something, or don't think you're serious about doing it, or don't understand that it will be of value. In those cases, if you show them a result, they can judge the result on its merits, not based on their assumptions. I did these projects because I enjoyed them. As it turned out, doing the projects provided a good background for my next career move.

NATURE OF THE WORK

Information Brokering

After two years I left CareerTrack to start my own company, Working Knowledge. The career move was unplanned — I hadn't "always dreamed of running my own business." Rather, the move to become an information broker actually evolved out the work I was doing at CareerTrack to develop the seminars. The structure of CareerTrack is such that the speakers are independent contractors: they present workshops for CareerTrack but most of them also run their own companies and present seminars on their own. Trainers started asking me to help them do research to develop their own seminars (essentially doing for them what I was doing for CareerTrack). That led me to realize that I could offer this service as a business. The appealing aspect of the idea was that research and writing were my favorite parts of the CareerTrack job, and here was a chance to expand that favorite part into a full-time job.

So, I founded Working Knowledge in 1988. The majority of my initial clients were speakers and trainers who wanted help developing their training programs or wanted to write a book but didn't have the time. I helped them by doing research for their books or seminars. My biggest client initially was Tom Peters, (co-author of *In Search of Excellence*) for whom I did company case studies. I had met Tom while at CareerTrack, because I wrote the curriculum to convert his books into a one-day seminar format. After I left CareerTrack, I gave the Tom Peters Group a call to say I wouldn't be at the upcoming meeting and to let them know I was off on my own. By a great stroke of luck, Tom was about to start on his next book and needed a researcher. They asked if I would be interested, and needless to say, I said "Yes!!"

It was a great project to work on: I did literature searches to identify companies that would fit the criteria Tom was looking for, conducted telephone and on-site interviews with the companies, and then wrote the case studies. I enjoyed doing these case studies — it was exciting to research companies, learn about what they were doing, and then pass that information along to others. I started focusing on this area as my specialty.

To those of you considering starting your own information brokering business, I'd suggest having a specific focus or niche that you offer as your specialty. The reason to specialize is twofold. First, it lets you more clearly describe what services you offer. Saying you're an "information broker" meets with many blank stares, so you'll often need to describe what you do in more detail. Having a specialty means that you can concretely describe what services you offer. Second, having a specialty builds your proficiency in the area, making subsequent assignments easier and better because of your accumulated background knowledge.

Personal Interest Becomes Basis for Non-Traditional Job

In the course of doing research for others, and because of my own intrinsic interest, I began developing a database of information for my own use. The database, called HyperThink, was a place where I collected and organized my notes on topics of interest to me: company examples, management development, R&D, organizational learning, and knowledge management. I'd read books or articles or attend conferences and take notes on the interesting information I learned. Then, I put the information into HyperThink. HyperThink is created in Hypercard on the Macintosh. It functions like an electronic stack of index cards, with the advantage that I can do Boolean searches and flexibly pull together information in new ways.

HyperThink served as a useful tool for me for client work. For example, a client would ask, "I give workshops on the importance of teamwork. Do you know of any good examples or stories of companies where self-directed teams have been instrumental in the company's success?" I would do a search on HyperThink and quickly pull together information for the client. In short, HyperThink was a tool I used to help me do a better job. I didn't think much about it until one day, when talking with a client, I mentioned HyperThink. The client was intrigued and wanted to know more. He asked if he could bring some colleagues over to see the system. Suddenly, I realized that this tool itself was interesting to clients. So, I began to include descriptions of HyperThink when talking with potential clients.

In turn, having HyperThink came to be the reason I was able to get a contract with the Massachusetts Institute of Technology in July 1995. The MIT Sloan School had started a research initiative called, "Inventing the Organizations of the 21st Century." Part of the mission of this research program was to identify and catalog examples of "new species" of companies. Thomas W. Malone, the Patrick J. McGovern Professor of Information Science at MIT and director of the Center for Coordination Science, had heard about my database and case study work I had done for

Tom Peters. He called me to discuss the possibility of my working on the Interesting Organizations Database for the initiative, to kick-start the project by getting a good set of companies into the database quickly as a foundation for later research.

Another natural outgrowth of my work has been to think a great deal about knowledge management. I've had to think about knowledge management for the sake of my business. (The better able I am to manage information and knowledge in my business, the better and faster service I can provide my clients.) As I mentioned above, I've now found that when I mention HyperThink, people are interested in that tool. People and companies are having to manage so much information now that the process of knowledge management is becoming a job function (Chief Knowledge Officer) in and of itself.

Knowledge Management

So, the next stage of my business (if I can actually predict a stage) will be to focus on the area of knowledge management. Joining me in this endeavor is my husband, Dana, an R&D engineer who has been developing software architectures for clients and is the person who developed the software for HyperThink. In 1995, we made Working Knowledge into a partnership (from a sole proprietorship) and began offering knowledge management consulting and systems. Growing this newer side of the business will proceed as it has in the past — giving presentations at conferences and writing articles and white papers — to let others know what we've learned in this area and how they might benefit from the ideas, experiences and tools, we've developed.

POINTERS FOR ACHIEVING SUCCESS

In choosing your specialty or niche, the most important factor is to choose an area in which you're intrinsically interested. If you specialize in your favorite areas, you'll not only be paid to work at your hobby, but you'll be intrinsically motivated to increase your knowledge in that area whether you're being paid or not. For example, I love reading about companies taking innovative action. Even when not on assignment, I read business journals and take notes on things like Acer's new expansion strategy or why Merck has been so successful developing new drugs. At a later date, these pieces of information may get used in client requests (such as "examples of successful R&D" or "examples of strategies for global expansion") or they may be woven into a longer written report or article.

Researching and writing isn't just what I do; it is part of who I am. If you can align your job with your values and interests, you'll be much more effective, valuable, and happy. You'll be able to offer your clients much more of value because of all the background knowledge you will have developed over the years of pursuing your personal interests. Moreover, the more you know, the more you can use and learn, and then the more you know—it's a virtuous spiral of increasing your knowledge and value.

Finally, having this focus means that most other information brokers aren't your competitors because it's unlikely that everyone's specialty will be identical. Rather, they're partners to whom you can refer clients when you get an inquiry for services that aren't your specialty. I have a personal network of "associates" like this, and it works to everyone's advantage: I don't have to accept an assignment out of my element, but I can still help the client by being able to refer him or her to someone else who has expertise in the area. Also, I'm eager to hear about others whose work is similar to mine, because we can refer clients to each other in times of overflow business.

Throughout my career, I've tried to take the favorite part of my current job and expand it, to get to do more of it. That goal—of getting paid to do what you enjoy—is much more attainable than people realize. It leads down a path that's unpredictable but interesting and logically connected.

To summarize, my new work tends to evolve out of my previous work. Therefore, the most important piece of advice I can offer is do work that you enjoy, so that you can become proficient at it and get to do more of it. Building on the skills you enjoy using and the topics you enjoy following means that you'll be able to have a rewarding career, regardless of whether the career is "traditional" or not.

Andrea Meyer
Working Knowledge
515 Forest Ave.
Boulder, CO 80304-2550
Tel: 303/440-0920; Fax: 303/449-3497
Email: meyerwk@workingknowledge.com

CHAPTER 17

ARRANGING EXCHANGES AMONG LIBRARIANS AROUND THE WORLD

JUDITH SIESS
President of Information Bridges International

INTRODUCTION

After 16 years as a librarian, I am now the president (and for now the sole employee) of Information Bridges International, a brand-new company specializing in arranging exchanges between libraries and librarians around the world. I also plan on doing some teaching, writing, and consulting. I have been a member of the Special Libraries Association since 1980. I was the first chair of the SOLO Librarian's Division of the Special Libraries Association, now the fifth largest division in the association at over 1000 members and have served at the chapter, division, and association level. (SOLO librarians are librarians working alone in an organization, without professional peers.) My first book, *The SOLO Librarian's Sourcebook*, has just been published by Information Today, Inc., and two others are in process.

As is common with librarians, I came to librarianship as a second career. I think I always wanted to be a librarian— maybe I was even destined to become one. In fact, the librarians at the Urbana (IL) Free Library helped to pick out my name. I started reading by the time I was three and had my library card at four. I worked in my grade school and junior high libraries. After graduating from Beloit College (a small liberal arts college in the Midwest where, as a true child of the sixties, I got a BA in Anthropology), I worked as "Research Librarian" for an urban planning firm. I ran a small, Solo library. Although I had had no formal training, years of working in and using libraries (including the great library at the University of Illinois at Urbana-Champaign), helped me to do a fairly creditable job of reclassifying the book collection and doing reference. It was here in Memphis, Tennessee, that I discovered my first special library — the Business and Technical Library of the Memphis Public Library. These wonderful folks would look up information for me and, if it was too extensive to provide over the phone, put the appropriate books out and open for me to consult when I came in. This was a good introduction to quality patron service.

After another few years of being sidetracked (marriage, a Master's in Anthropology, divorce, and several years as a secretary), I wound up in Champaign, Illinois, my home town. I worked as a statistical assistant to a price forecasting group in the department of Agricultural Economics at the University of Illinois. For my work, I needed constant access to data. I found out there was an Agricultural Economics Reference Room. Despite its name, it was merely an unorganized collection of U. S. Department of Agriculture bulletins and statistics. I asked if I could take charge of it, and the department said yes. At about the same time I met Chuck Davis (at bowling, of all places), then dean of the Graduate School of Library and Information Science. He encouraged me to enroll in the Master's program, which I did. I used the Ag Econ Reference Room as a lab for my classwork in addition to my work for the department. I talked them into providing online searching for faculty and graduate students, and I developed a very primitive online catalog. I also founded the Agricultural Economics Reference Organization, which is still functioning with over 50 members at universities and other agricultural libraries throughout the world.

Since I knew that I wanted to work in a sci-tech library after graduation, I tailored my coursework appropriately. I took sci-tech reference, online searching, abstracting and indexing, statistical methods, government documents, special libraries, and cataloging. I also did a thesis on "Information Needs and Information-Gathering Behavior of Research Engineers." I had a wonderful time doing the research and learned a lot about how engineers approach (or don't approach) information and libraries. My advisor was Professor Linda Smith, who remains a mentor and friend. The basis for my thesis research was an internship at the U.S. Army Corps of Engineers Construction Engineering Research Laboratory in Champaign. I went there one day a week for a summer, learning about the collection, answering reference questions, and shadowing their librarian, the late Martha Blake. I have always said that I learned 95% of what I know about being a good librarian from Martha. She provided excellent customer service and worked very closely with the engineers. They adored her. I knew then what being a librarian was all about and have always strived to make her proud of me. I try to get back to Urbana-Champaign at least once a year to talk to the students about "Life in the Real World — What They Don't Teach You in Library School."

After receiving my MS in LIS in 1982, I went job hunting. My first professional position was—surprise—a SOLO library. (Note: I found this job through the ASIS placement service at their annual meeting.) I was hired to start a library for a small (15 people) biotechnology company in Ashland, Ohio. Since the president's wife was a librarian, he understood the importance of information for research and development. Since I had never started a library before and knew absolutely nothing about enzymology, I turned to the librarians at the University of Illinois. The chemistry and biology librarians were very helpful in suggesting basic reference books and journals to purchase and general guidelines for establishing a scientific library.

After three years in Ashland, the company downsized, and the library was closed. I moved on to Cleveland and worked for a friend who was establishing his own biotechnology company. I was secretary, administrative assistant, researcher, office manager, and librarian. It was good experience, but not exactly what I had in mind. I got back to library work by subbing for a librarian on maternity leave from a contract chemical research facility. They had a good reference collection, and I used the three months to familiarize myself with various online services and reference books. I moved on to another maternity leave situation, this time at NASA Lewis Research Center. It featured an even better collection, many librarians to learn from, and interesting reference work, but it still was not what I wanted. Finally, I got call from the SLA Cleveland Chapter placement officer about a job at Bailey Controls Company. I had seen the ad and figured I was overqualified since it did not require a degree. The placement officer assured me that it was just what I was looking for, so I applied and got the job.

My tenure at Bailey (now Elsag Bailey Process Automation) was interesting, challenging, frustrating, rewarding, and nearly everything I could have asked for—at least for the first seven years. I was the only information provider for what became a $2 billion company with over 10,000 employees in the United States, Europe, Asia, the Mid-East, and South America. At the beginning, it was a typical library. I had about 2500 books, 2500 standards, and 100 journal subscriptions. There was a card catalog. I purchased books and subscriptions for all 1000 employees at their Cleveland, Ohio, headquarters and some field staff. Most of the time was spent on acquisitions and circulation, with some online searching and interlibrary loan. When I left, it had only about 600 books, the same 2500 standards, about 25 journal subscriptions, and several CD-ROM products.

The card catalog was gone, replaced by a networked online catalog. Most of my time was spent on competitive intelligence, producing a weekly *Executive Intelligence Report* and a monthly newsletter, sent to top management and marketing personnel worldwide via e-mail and fax and posted on the company's World Wide Web home page.

Why did I leave such a "good" job? The company was changing, my job was changing, and my attitude was changing. I didn't think they were going in the right direction—or at least the direction I wanted to take. The company's emphasis was on departmental fiscal responsibility, and my department was increasingly reluctant to pay me to provide services for other departments. I charged out my out-of-pocket costs, but the department paid my salary and overhead. My boss wanted me to focus on providing information via the World Wide Web, especially competitor information on the systems area. This took me away from reference and bibliographic instruction (mostly on Internet or the WWW), which I loved. Resources were increasingly scarce, and I felt I couldn't provide the level of service I wanted. In addition, I wanted more free time for travel and family.

NATURE OF THE WORK

I had wanted to leave Elsag for about a year, but knew I shouldn't retire without something to retire to. In 1996 I found something that piqued my interest enough to base a career on—I hope. The first glimmer of an idea came when a consultant, Jean Graef, said she had a client who was starting a corporate library and had hired a "librarian" without a library degree. Since there was no library school anywhere near, the company thought an internship and library visits arranged by me might substitute.

An interesting idea, but I turned Jean down since I felt the client should hire a degreed librarian instead. Next, Guy St. Clair invited me to join the People-to-People Citizen Ambassador Mission to the Republic of South Africa on Information Management and Specialized Libraries that he was organizing. I accepted immediately since I had always wanted to visit that country. He explained to me that one of the concerns of the South Africans was getting overseas training for their librarians. In preparation for the trip I talked to Hannelore Rader, then head of the Cleveland State University Library, who had just returned from South Africa. She agreed with Guy that this was a very pressing need. I began to think that this might be an interesting business. The last piece of the puzzle came when I volunteered to serve as Chair of the International Relations Committee for the Science-

Technology Division of SLA. The Association International Relations Committee was going to focus on the need for internships and mentors for SLA members outside the U.S.

After returning from South Africa, inspired by the enthusiasm educators and librarians there expressed for my idea, I "retired" from Elsag in December 1996 and formed Information Bridges International (IBI). The mission of IBI is two-fold. My primary goal is to facilitate exchanges of library personnel among libraries around the world, including librarians outside the United States who wish to visit or work temporarily in the United States or other countries; librarians in the United States who wish to visit or work temporarily in other countries; library students (especially outside the United States) seeking internships; and librarians (especially outside the United States) seeking one-on-one mentoring relationships with other librarians.

The services I will provide include matching of visitors with appropriate libraries, advice and assistance with housing and travel, and continuing contact with both host and visitor to assure a mutually beneficial professional experience. I will initially focus on special libraries, expanding to national and academic libraries and then public libraries and schools of library and information science.

The second mission is to facilitate networking among librarians, both within and outside the United States, especially to SOLO and newly qualified librarians, by making them aware of existing formal or informal networks and/or helping to establish a network in their home country where none exists.

Although I do not want to spend a lot of time teaching the Internet—it is far too difficult to keep current—I will be teaching several courses for my former employer. In fact, one reason I left there is that people kept asking me to teach these courses, but my boss wouldn't let me. I enjoy teaching, people say I am good at it, and there is a desperate need at Elsag for this kind of training. My husband, who is a self-employed accountant, also has several clients who have expressed a need for Internet classes. I am also developing a course based on my book, *The SOLO Librarian's Sourcebook*, which I hope to teach at SLA conferences, library schools, and elsewhere. Patricia Ricci, the author of *Standards: A Resource and Guide for Identification, Selection, and Acquisition*, has "given" the book to me, and I plan to revise and enlarge it and republish it. I will also retool the course I teach based on the book and try to expand the market for it beyond librarians to other users of standards (engineers, contractors, even students).

The most vexing problem I have with starting IBI is figuring how to charge for my services. Making money is not my primary interest (helping others is), but I need to live. I am considering not-for-profit status for part of the company and seeking grants to help pay the expenses of arranging visits. I plan to charge $50 or actual costs (whichever is less) for setting up a mentoring relationship over the Internet and $55 per hour (plus travel expenses) for other consulting. The biggest problem is the pricing of seminars or classes. I know that others charge $700 or more for similar classes, but this seems very high to me. (I wouldn't pay that much myself.) Somewhere in the $250-450 area is where I'll probably wind up. Since the survey done by the SLA Science-Technology International Relations Committee has formed a substantial part of my thinking and will be used for marketing, I plan to offer a 10% discount for members of the Special Libraries Association.

I am contemplating creating a Board of Advisors for IBI. I would ask special, academic, and public librarians and library educators from the U. S. and overseas to be available to advise me on the best way to serve my potential customers. I have had some interest from librarians in South Africa and Australia in serving on the Board. At present I do not have a WWW page. Many of my prospective clientele do not even have e-mail, much less access to the web. I imagine I will develop one in the future, however.

How is it going? I have found a lot of interest in what I'm doing. I haven't advertised at all yet. Between people seeing my "10-second commercial" (arranging exchanges among libraries and librarians around the world) in my signature online and inquiring as to the nature of my business and my passing out business cards at library conferences and meetings, the word is getting out. In fact, I have more potential customers than I can handle right now. I haven't earned any money yet (February), but I am still getting organized. I work one day a week at Elsag (doing some research and reference and closing down the library), so there is money coming in. I will begin teaching an Internet course there on March, 20, 1997.

I am working out of my home, so setup expenses have been minimal so far. I purchased a new printer-fax-scanner and upgraded my computer ($1200 total) and had business cards designed and printed. (The bridge logo was inspired by one I saw on the road between Johannesburg and

Pretoria South Africa and is in partial tribute to my dad, a former bridge engineer.) I have finished my book and completed some other writing for library journals. So far, life is good and I expect it only to get better.

POINTERS FOR ACHIEVING SUCCESS

What do you need to succeed as an entrepreneur? You first need courage, and enthusiasm, belief in and commitment to what you are doing. You will need marketing skills, people skills, and presentation skills. You must be a self-starter, and you must be able to organize yourself and your surroundings.

Do a market study before going into business—make sure someone wants what you want to provide—and is willing to pay for it. However, you must find a need, fill it, and then figure out how to make a living from it. Don't start with "I need to make money"—that will doom you to failure, or at least mediocrity. Don't be afraid to ask for help. Talk to people in similar businesses. Most will be willing to answer general questions. Form alliances with other businesses that complement yours. (I am working with a business research company that wants to offer their customers the option of hosting a foreign librarian to gain insight into other countries' economies.)

Advertise, but do it intelligently and professionally. (I do not suggest "spamming" library lists on the Internet.) Use your networking skills to make potential customers aware of your service. Be confident in your abilities and your idea. Don't be impatient for success and don't get discouraged.

And finally, enjoy yourself! Life is about more than making money. (After all, if worse comes to worse, you can always get a —ugh—job.)

Judith Siess
Information Bridges International
477 Harris Road
Richmond Heights, OH 44143
Tel/Fax: 216/486-7443
E-mail: jsiess@en. com

CHAPTER 18

REVERSE CAREER PATH: LIBRARY MANAGER TO ENVIRONMENTAL INFORMATION RESEARCHER

BARBARA L. WAGNER
Proprietor of The Access Point (TAP)

INTRODUCTION

I started my career about three decades ago, working at the Winchester (Massachusetts) Public Library. Along the way I received the A.B. in Biology from Heidelberg College, the M.S. in Library Science from Western Reserve University, and a Certificate of Advanced Studies in Environmental Information from the University of Denver. During that time I held some information management positions not based in libraries.

My career as an information person developed as I took advantage of the options and opportunities available at key points in my life. But I had a clear goal, and the choices I made at those points were calculated to move me toward it. And while my goal evolved over the years, my approach remained the same: to incorporate as much of my experience and education as possible in whatever came next. In other words, I did not want to waste the time I had invested along the way.

I started with a plan to combine academic training in biology with library-science skills, and work in specialized libraries. This idea was not based on experience, since I had worked as a laboratory assistant rather than a library clerk during college. But I loved books and libraries. My motivation was heightened by a tour of the Eli Lilly Technical Library, which I took between pursuing graduate courses in microbiology and starting library school at Western Reserve University. After a decade of practical library experience in reference and management, I returned to library school. At the University of Denver, I attended the sixth-year program to specialize in environmental information.

At this point I started my career as an environmental information specialist, which coincided with the rise of the environmental movement.

About the time of the first Earth Day, I decided to go to DU. I knew by then that I loved connecting people with the information they needed—a love that has endured throughout my career. I have to believe that if the people have the environmental information they need to made solid, wise decisions, then the Earth and her creatures will be more likely to survive.

In the 1970s, the need to get information to the public expanded opportunities in environmental agencies. I utilized contacts and knowledge gained from my work running the Fish and Wildlife Reference Service to become an information transfer specialist with the U.S. Fish and Wildlife Service (USFWS). In this position, I worked with project scientists to plan the products resulting from their contracts. During this time I married, and my son Douglas was born, I commuted three hours daily, helped remodel a house, and also served as Chairperson of the SLA Natural Resources Division. From the USFWS job in Fort Collins, I became an information scientist at the Solar Energy Research Institute (SERI) near Denver. In 1981 when SERI laid off 60% of their workforce, demolishing the Inquiry and Referral ServicesBranch, I launched the information business I had been planning for several years: The Access Point (TAP). I operated TAP on a part-time basis through 1995.

The following year, 1982, I landed a reference and researcher job in the University of Wyoming's Science and Geology Libraries. Then followed five years of managing the Colorado State Publications Library, and getting its catalog running on the CARL system.

During this time I continued consulting part-time, so TAP moved with me. Throughout my career I took advantage of every workshop, conference session, and exhibit that could add skills useful in my business. These included marketing, publicity, and new-technology demonstrations. Also, I branched out by becoming certified as a records manager. I paid for my own professional memberships and many conferences. I considered all this continual education to be investing in my own career, because what I learned stayed with me.

A long-hoped-for chance to become the Denver regional librarian for the U.S. Environmental Protection Agency got me back on track. But within a couple years, my plan to make this a long-term commitment was thwarted, and instead I had the opportunity to gain experience in computer security and systems analysis. The chance to direct a library attracted me to the U. S. Geological Survey Denver Regional Library, which rounded out my natural resources experience.

In view of the government downsizing trend, I determined that 1996 was the year to expand The Access Point to a full-time consulting business. So I took an early "retirement" and implemented my plan of a life-after-government second career.

NATURE OF THE WORK

The Access Point is a Denver-based information services company offering research, information management consulting, technical and business writing and editing, plus Internet training. TAP specializes in environmental information research. A lone eagle—as I call myself—I operate TAP as a sole proprietorship from my home office. Providing information services through TAP is different every week and every day. Each project, contract, or assignment I undertake for clients has new elements. I use the research, writing, and training skills developed over many years of experience, and the knowledge gained in classes and in life to be successful. But how that experience is applied in consulting varies according to the nature of the task. It is important to keep an open mind and to use a creative approach to solving the information problem at hand, rather than assuming that a traditional library-science solution is the most appropriate. Most times, TAP's clients do not want to hear that the answer was not in the book, library, or files searched. They also tend not to need to know how the information was found: they just want to receive what they asked for, on or before deadline.

In conducting environmental information research, The Access Point searches technical and business literature, legal sources, land and property records, and provides library support. For this research, TAP accesses library sources, databases, the Internet, and community resources, and also contacts experts to supplementthese sources.

TAP's writing and editing services include technical articles, reports and abstracts, business reports, marketing materials such as fliers and pamphlets, news releases and public service announcement text. In doing my writing, I give consideration to the readers' knowledge, background, and experiences, as well as the intended function of the article or report.

As a spin-off from research, TAP now offers Internet and computer tutoring, and consults on website development. Presentations are also made on efficiently finding information via the Internet. For training, TAP starts with the level of knowledge, interests, and the applications the students plan to make of the skills they are learning.

The information management consulting services TAP provides include organization of libraries, design and layout of information centers, and consulting on issues. For all the consulting work, I tap into my network of colleagues in libraries, information centers, and in resource agencies. My professional association work, particularly as a president of the SLA Rocky Mountain Chapter, has been instrumental in developing helpful contacts and networking skills. Now my participation in Colorado Information Professionals Network and the Association of Independent Information Professionals contributes to my business.

Most consulting projects require a combination of research, writing, and clear communications. Communication is probably the most important element in consulting, as it is in reference work within a library. Two essentials are establishing a clear understanding of the work to be done and the limitations imposed by client directions and consultant's abilities, and giving straightforward and clear feedback. The most valuable service TAP can offer is careful listening at the start and throughout a project.

Also essential is taking time for business operations tasks (e.g. promptly sending invoices); marketing to line up future business; and maintaining and expanding skills (especially computer-related ones) and knowledge (of sources, trends, business developments, laws and regulations). I have read that the work, marketing, and tending to business should each take one-third of an entrepreneur's time. However, making this work in practice can definitely be a challenge.

Qualifications

While a library degree is not required, curiosity and research skills are basic. My library-science and natural resources education and my information-management experience have given me the credentials and qualifications to be an information consultant. Other necessary qualifications are in the business areas of marketing, communications, organization, coordination, and financial management. The ability to juggle many concurrent tasks without getting confused, good health, and stamina are the same qualities needed in library-based reference work. Motivation is paramount when becoming an entrepreneur; one needs more than skills to carry it through.

Commitment to high-quality service and positive attitudes are mandatory, as is the recognition that I cannot afford to "give away the store." I also cannot afford to take the time to explore peripheral research leads instead of marketing the business (even on the web). Some would-be consultants say they just want to do the research, not the marketing. They will not be successful unless they work for a company that lines up clients for them. I need to focus on what I can get paid for, rather than on how I might rather spend my time. Thinking like a private investigator is useful; acting like a bureaucrat is not.

The freelancing experts tell us to find a niche. A Renaissance woman of many interests has difficulty staying in a niche. Environmental research is my solution because it covers the waterfront (and a lot of other fronts, as well). The nature of this environmental beast is fragmentation, multiplicity of sources, cross-discipline work, and conflicting views. My work at TAP is a challenge, sometimes frustrating, but always interesting, never boring.

Pros and Cons

The advantages of running my own information services business are having the freedom to do my work as I think best, and finding many opportunities to try creative ways to provide TAP's services. The empowerment I feel to control my own life, to choose my associates, and my work environment, is a reward in itself. My past experiences have given me the necessary skills and judgment, and prepared me for this new lifestyle.

The disadvantages include less financial security, a fluctuating income, and no steady paychecks. However, a consultant may feel more secure in some respects: having a number of client-employers means that if one drops out, others are still furnishing some income. An uncertain and unpredictable future can be worrisome, but so can the threat of corporate downsizing and budget cuts. Keeping overhead low and managing cash flow are much more urgent concerns for an entrepreneur. Having to explain to potential clients, and even to some librarians, what an information consultant does can be a challenge too. Some find creating structure to their workday to be difficult after working in organizations: I do not have this problem.

The total responsibility for achieving success can be, at the same time, both a positive and a negative for the freelance librarian. But then, success may be defined in different ways. For me, success is supporting myself through TAP, plus seeing some balance in my life among work, family, and personal pursuits. My goal is to continue working at what I love and making a contribution to society. I expect the future frosting on this cake will be some leisure to travel, take walks, read, pursue hobbies, play with my grandson Andy, and relax with a cup of tea and a cat on my lap. But I will always be working on some project, perhaps writing books.

POINTERS FOR ACHIEVING SUCCESS

Carpe diem. And figure out how to make lemonade when life presents lemons. Taking an entrepreneurial attitude and outlook is important to achieving success. Pat Wagner once said I was the most entrepreneurial librarian she had met. I was influenced at a young age by *The Power of Positive Thinking*. Seeing possibilities in problems and difficult situations pays off by opening new doors and directions for my career. Also continual education—learning new skills all the time—provides a solid basis for TAP's training services and makes me worth consulting.

Meeting client's deadlines can wreak havoc with my personal life. Information consultants joke about trying to have a life apart from their businesses. I find that, while my appointment book must constantly be at hand, more entries are entered in pencil. Flexibility, responsiveness, and adjusting my plans to fit around the needs of TAP's clients have proven to be very important. Understanding and supportive friends and relatives are a real treasure: I am fortunate to have both.

The monicker "lone eagle" mentioned at the start of this chapter fits me. Also, it helps being a self-starter, a morning person, analytical, decisive, an extrovert, and at least somewhat organized. Being a firstborn sibling and an Aries probably helps too. I function much better not being hemmed-in by a bureaucratic environment.

A plaque I received from my sister, Coral Lee Wagner Willson, sums up my working life: "A man travels the world over in search of life's meaning and returns home to find it." So said the sage, Benjamin Franklin, and I am sure he included women in this observation. My home-based business, The Access Point, is part of my life's meaning and is my gift to the Earth.

Barbara L. Wagner
The Access Point
PO Box 280038
Lakewood, CA 80228-0038
Tel: 303/274-5309; Fax: 303/274-6103
E-mail: blwagner@tap.com
Web page: http://www.tap.com/tap

CHAPTER 19

COMBINING SOFTWARE DESIGNING WITH ACADEMIC CONSULTING

SCOTT WYANT
Director at Spinoza Ltd.

INTRODUCTION

I am the director of information science for a small software development firm and also serve as an information technology consultant for Antioch University, both located in Los Angeles, California. In addition I run my own information systems consulting firm. So I am both an employee and an entrepreneur. Perhaps it may be surprising, but, despite my complete absorption in different phases of information science and technology for many years, in reality information science is actually my third or fourth career. I have had some unusual jobs.

As a junior high school student, I spent a lot of time at the public library—partly because I liked it, and partly because it was a place that I could go that was out of my parent's line-of-sight. The library always seemed like a refuge to me, even while I was being shushed. For several reasons I never really considered librarianship as a career for myself. For one thing, I thought I was too much of a noise-maker to be an effective "shusher." To my young eye, that seemed to be a big part of the job. So you can see why it took me a while even to consider entering a library school.

Like many people my age (I'm 45), I wandered through college without any clear idea of what I wanted to do with the rest of my life. After my first stint in college (I left in 1973, eight credits short of a degree), I moved around the country a bit, working at odd jobs including drafting, photography, and writing. I had a brief brush with glory when I did some drawings for a member of the University of California—Irvine chemistry department, who had discovered that freon was burning a hole in the ozone layer. This was 1974, his name was Sherry Rowland, and he won the 1995

Nobel Prize for that discovery. I like to think my meticulous draftsmanship was a contributing factor.

In 1975, I fell in love with the woman who (eventually) became my wife. The day after Christmas, we loaded some belongings into a 1963 Dodge Dart and took off for Mexico and points south. Among the belongings was a crate filled with about 100 books, including a two-volume *Funk and Wagnal's Dictionary*. After six months, we had a choice--to go back to the United States, or to sell everything, including the car, and keep going south. We liquidated and crossed over into Guatemala. I should add that I did not sell the dictionary, and continued to lug it around in my bag. It was by far the heaviest thing I owned! We settled in the beautiful town of San Lucas Toliman, on the shores of Lake Atitlan.

At this point I was writing the occasional travel article, teaching Spanish to traveling Americans and English to some of the young people in San Lucas. I discovered that I loved teaching, and told myself that when we returned to the U.S., I was going to finish my B.A. degree and get a teaching credential. It was another year before we finally ran completely out of money and wended our way back to the States. I didn't get a teaching credential. Instead, I worked in restaurants, managed to pick up the credits I needed for my B.A., and then literally fell into television, where I worked for nearly a decade. My very first job was a real eye-opener, though the pay was miserable. I was a fact checker for a quiz show called "The Joker's Wild." The writer wrote a question using whatever source he had at hand, and I had to verify each and every word in the question with two other sources—very much a reference librarian sort of job! And if I made a mistake, I could bet that one of the 5 or 6 million people who watched the show would notice it and let me know.

How I Became a Librarian

My next career change came while I was on a plane to Orlando, where I was supposed to write and co-produce 35 half-hour television shows in five days. That is an almost completely impossible and inhuman schedule, and my wife was back home in Santa Monica with our month-old daughter. I had picked up a copy of Stewart Brand's new book *The Media Lab* to read on the plane. By the time we landed, I had finished the book and made up my mind. After a hellish week in Florida, I flew home, slept for three days and applied to the UCLA Graduate School of Library and Information Science—it was the closest thing to the MIT Media Lab I could find anywhere near my home. I was accepted for admission in September of 1989.

At that time, the UCLA GSLIS program was really two programs under one roof—the traditional librarianship program, and the information science wing. Integration was uneasy, and after the required core courses, most students chose one path or the other. I'm still not sure why, but I did my best to pick the cream of both, and I'm very glad I did. As a result, I have a much better background in cataloging and classification theory than most information scientists, and much greater computer and information theory training than most traditional librarians. And that makes me much more employable. I have noted that UCLA and a few other library and information science programs are eliminating cataloging as a requirement. From my perspective, this is a mistake. I'd encourage anyone entering the field to get a good grasp of cataloging fundamentals.

NATURE OF THE WORK

After graduating from UCLA, my first job was as a consultant to AND Communications, a multimedia publishing company. At the time AND was selling a number of educational laserdisks. I was hired to rationalize the structure of their databases. Essentially, this was a cataloging and classification task, but in a computer environment, and it was just what I'd studied in graduate school. I did similar jobs for other multimedia companies, including the one that produced a compact-disk-interactive version of the TV show "Jeopardy." Late in 1991, I was contacted by Antioch University, Los Angeles (through the career office at UCLA). They were creating a position called "Instructional Resources Coordinator." The job entailed running a computer lab, connecting the university to whatever electronic information resources they could afford, and training faculty and staff on the then-brand-new Internet. I took the job, which turned out to be great for me because I got to do lots of teaching.

It's often said that teaching is the best way to learn something, and it's surely true for me. When I took the job, I had barely even touched a Macintosh computer. Today, much of my consulting work is Mac-based. In 1991, the only layperson's explanation of the Internet was *Zen and the Art of the Internet*—which was only available on the Internet, via ftp! So I had to teach myself everything before I could pass the information on to the faculty and staff.

How I Got My Current Job

In 1993, again courtesy of UCLA, I was contacted by a startup company with the intriguing name of Origami Inc. They sent me a job description which read, in part, "LIBRARY SCIENTIST: UNIQUE OPPORTUNITY! Small startup company on the cutting edge of the digital information revolution seeks an intelligent, self-motivated library scientist with an affinity for technology to help us deconstruct and redesign information into new, more intelligent forms." I was interviewed by two guys in shorts, who described to me a product called "The Reference Web." For the then-nascent hand-held computer market, The Reference Web would give people instant, real-time access to a broad spectrum of reference materials automatically linked to whatever text they were reading. It was an exciting idea, and my position would entail choosing the appropriate reference works, encoding them in SGML (Standard Generalized Markup Language), as well as generating original material.

It sounded like the best job in the world, and I took it. I found a person to fill my position at Antioch University, and maintained a consulting relationship with the school.

Then my career took another twist. As we all know now, the hand-held computer did not take the world by storm in 1993, or in 1994. We found ourselves developing a really cool product for a market that had basically ceased to exist. So, we did a mid-air twist. The programmers with whom I work (we were still just a three-person shop) proposed that we create a couple of "chip-shot" products that could buy us time, and pay the rent until we could do a complete shift of direction. They had experience in creating tools for software developers, so we designed some tools for programmers who used Microsoft's Visual Basic programming language. My job? Documentation, customer support, and marketing.

We renamed our company Spinoza Ltd. (R.I.P. Origami) and set to work. My problem was that I knew absolutely nothing about Visual Basic. The tools we were creating were fairly complex, and in order to document them, I had to know how they worked. So, I had to teach myself how to program in Visual Basic, quite a stretch for a guy who had always been a software and hardware user, not much accustomed to peering under the hood.

It took me about three months to become somewhat competent, though I'll never be a "real" programmer. For anyone who wants to learn the rudiments of programming, Visual Basic is great. It's also possible to build very useful applications using Visual Basic, though the language will never be as elegant and efficient as, say, C++. We finished our products, put them in the marketplace, and enjoyed a small amount of success. Our big break came when a software giant that I cannot name bought a chunk of our code for a ton of money. They then included that code in one of their own products. That infusion of cash enabled us to turn our attention back to the consumer market.

We're now prototyping a new kind personal information manager that the world has never seen, and about which I cannot be more specific right now. Trust me—when we finish with it, you'll want it. I'm in on the design, I am doing all the research, and I'm the in-house guinea pig. I'll also be running the beta test program on the out-of-house guinea pigs. I'm designing the website, which will be unlike any other website you've seen. Add to this the intellectual stimulus I'm receiving as part of the Antioch community, and my work life is quite full and rich.

POINTERS FOR ACHIEVING SUCCESS

In general, I'd say I've been lucky in my career ever since I made the decision to go back to graduate school. I'm sure I made the right decision in combining traditional library training (i.e., cataloging, classification, and reference work) with all the information science. While I was in graduate school, I worked part-time at the Beverly Hills Public Library, at the reference desk in the arts department. That experience, too, was invaluable. Among other things, I found out that there was more to being a librarian than "shushing" kids. I also remember thinking that there were many worse jobs in the world than being a librarian in a small town library.

My advice to anyone who wants to have a career like mine? There's no such thing as too much education. There's no substitute for personal relationships. Practice writing, because it's going to be the way we communicate with each other for a long time. And do one thing that I have yet to do--take art and design classes. Web pages can be deadly dull when they're done badly.

Scott Wyant
Director of Information Science
Spinoza Ltd.
11333 Iowa Ave.
Los Angeles, CA 90230
Fax: 310/815-8780 (home)
E-mail: scott-wyant@loop.com

Part Three

Special Library Education for the New Millenium

CHAPTER 20

A VIRTUAL LIBRARIAN IN ACADEMIC MEDICINE

JEANNE TIFFT
Association Of American Medical Colleges

INTRODUCTION

I returned to the United States in 1983, after years of living and raising children in developing countries overseas, eager to build a midlife career. I'd decided not to take the six years or so necessary to earn a doctorate in history of art (my youthful MA was then 25 years out of date) but rather to do an 18-month MLS I thought I'd learn to run a library instead of a museum.

After earning the MLS in 1984, I spent eleven years on a long term institutional contract with a research and reference service supporting the worldwide staff of the U.S. Agency for International Development. I began behind the reference desk, became a research analyst, transformed a moribund document collection into a humming Development Information Center, led a strategic planning process, transformed myself into the organization Internet expert, and finished as senior advisor looking around for the next step.

A Virtual Library

I was invited to create a "virtual library," at first, briefly, at the National Research Council; then, since mid-1996, at the Association of American Medical Colleges (AAMC). I have a traditional job title, "AAMC Librarian," meant to reassure traditional users, while at the same time we implement a menu of virtual information services they might otherwise resist as unfamiliar, unnecessary, and uncomfortable. As we are only at the beginning, we must keep traditional and virtual versions of the same services going at once. For example, we distribute our journal tables of contents both as e-mail messages from our UnCover Reveal profile, and in a weekly photocopied publication we do ourselves, called *TOCWeek*. Users send us article requests from both formats.

Our goal is to manage AAMC knowledge assets electronically, making sources and services (both internally generated and externally acquired) accessible through everyone's desktop browser. AAMC is creating an intranet, in addition to its well-developed external World Wide Web site (http://www.aamc.org), which will make a virtual reference center possible. When varied resources and the pathways to them are available through a common interface—the browser, staff can be as self-sufficient as they want to be in information-seeking. I'm fortunate to have major management support and significant technical resources with which to re-define information, document, and knowledge management for this organization. Eventually we expect to impact the academic medicine community that AAMC leads.

NATURE OF THE WORK

Plans for the Reference Center

I began by combining the AAMC archives and AAMC library, both print-based traditional resources, into a unified reference center. I imagine it as analagous to a switching station with diagrams and maps. Here are some of our plans.

1. A small digital library of selected archive document sequences linked to their modern successors, thus bringing past and present experience together and making it readily available to staff.

2. A relational database of archival finding aids that references SGML-compatible descriptions, container lists, and accompanying and related materials.

3. A CD-ROM tower that I plan to populate with reference works used organization-wide.

4. A Z39.50-compatible OPAC that provides for distributed office collections of books, videotapes, audiotapes, journal and newsletter subscriptions, etc., in addition to a core collection of shared reference works and journals maintained in the Reference Center.

5. A document management system that provides for document life cycle management, from authorship to publication to archiving.

6. An online index to *Academic Medicine*, a journal more than 100 years old, only partially indexed in MEDLINE.

7. A highly tailored jump list to web resources regularly and heavily used by AAMC staff.

8. Site licenses for selected electronic resources heavily used by, or critical to the mission of, the organization.

We maintain traditional library technical services, but use the Internet and electronic methods as much as possible. We acquire cataloging data via ftp, deal with the serials jobber via e-mail, search library catalogs via telnet, and use databases for document delivery via the web.

What It Took

My entire work experience has been with multidisciplinary and knowledge-intensive organizations, and happened to coincide with the explosive spread first of the PC and then of the Internet. It was a steep learning curve. My life experience before 1983 was mostly in countries where the telephones did not work very well and the bow drill was still in active use. In such countries, though, everyone is intensely interested in usable information, as long as it is good for doing something with. That experience has stood me in good stead.

What I learned in library school has actually been less relevant, with one exception: a course in library administration. Its intellectually rigorous syllabus on the principles of organizational life and management has served me well in special librarianship. The technical basis: cataloging, database searching, computer programming, and so on, were necessary but not in themselves enough—though I thought all too many reading assignments strove to convince us to believe they were. Such tasks are now done by technical and support staff whom I have trained.

It was so necessary to acquire additional knowledge and develop additional skills that I took seminars and workshops and followed topics I rarely found seeping usefully into library literature: communications theory, strategic planning, database design, economics of information, and the information industry.

In retrospect, three areas were the most helpful in providing the knowledge, skills, and attitudes that prepared me to do what I'm doing now: service management, technology as a set of tools, and information as a communication process.

Service Management

Service management principles and methods identified and developed in industry settings do very well for information service management too, whether the largest library or the smallest individual broker. I was particularly inspired by some research on the attributes of quality and value that customers actually perceive in a service transaction, done by three professors of marketing at Texas A&M and Duke Universities. Their conclusions appeared in the *Sloan Management Review* in 1990: "Five imperatives for improving service quality."

These service imperatives are as follows.

- Something tangible that represents the intangible service
- Reliability (dependability and accuracy)
- Responsiveness (willingness, promptness)
- Assurance (knowledge and courtesy)
- Empathy (caring attention)
  Such attributes seemed worth developing in a reference service staff at all levels.

Doing so took using methods adapted from service marketing. I took the position that "marketing is concerned with getting and keeping customers," substituting "users" or "clients" for customers.(2) We learned how to do survey research and market segmentation, not merely to understand our user groups and their needs, but also to use that understanding in developing and delivering services that met those needs. This helped us correct erroneous assumptions about users' needs upon which earlier services had been based.

Many user studies have concluded that information-seeking occurs in the context of a situation or task the user is dealing with. Robert S. Taylor has called this a "use environment."(3)   We implemented this in practice by paying attention to the purposes, concerns, outputs, and deadline rhythms of various managers, staffs, and working groups.

As one way to understand these patterns, I learned how to do critical incident interviews for individuals and focus group interviews for work teams. We learned to treat the reference interview as both service encounter and helping interview. We trained staff in what Taylor calls "levels of question formation"(4) because we found that most requesters first present a question already unconsciously compromised by what the requester thinks might answer the information need.

Helping skills on the part of the interviewer become paramount to getting that need met. Accordingly we adapted and trained staff in specific interpersonal communication techniques as taught in medicine, law, and social work interviewing rather than librarianship.

Technology as a Set of Tools

The most useful PC application for any special library situation is whatever database package or macro available that can be designed to do two very important tasks: capture data on services performed, (with a lot less effort than it takes to do the work,) and to aggregate that data into indicators that make sense to management and stakeholders. The accountability this demonstrates is mandatory these days. I've used DBase, Excel spreadsheets, tally sheets, and sign-in books, to name a few. Right now I'm using a Groupwise macro that converts e-mail messages into request records.

A special librarian needs to understand some basics of database design, some elementary statistics, and a graphics package or two, as well as know how to give staff appropriate incentives to observe the necessary procedures and enter their request records.

The most useful Internet application I've found for any special library situation is whatever helps one's clientele use the Internet as a research resource. Organizations new to the Internet usually concern themselves first with dissemination of information. Research staffs are left to start with Yahoo! and then stumble around frustrated with not finding what they think they should be able to find. Depending on the technical infrastructure of one's organization and on the information seeking habits of one's clientele, there are many possible interventions a special librarian could make to help this clientele.

Information as Communication

I have come to imagine information as a communication process. Perhaps this is the most important thing I've learned in the past 12 years. To paraphrase Brenda Dervin, the communications scholar, information is not a thing like a brick to be thrown into a user's bucket.(5) John Perry Barlow even more humanistically, writes that "information is a relationship."(6) This approach is, I believe, key to a special library's success in its organization. The underlying assumption is that special librarians and clientele are collaborators in identifying and accessing what the client needs.

From the interpersonal, one-on-one event of a reference interview, to an announcement broadcast to all staff via e-mail, communication skills are paramount for a special librarian to ensure that information is conveyed in the manner, the terms, and at the time appropriate to the situation.

In practice, for example, an organization develops an accepted manner of using e-mail that suits its organizational culture. It is vital that the special library establish its appropriate place in that milieu and create an appropriate message consistently applied. I've found that e-mail exchanges with remote information requesters could, with care, be turned into good reference interviews or user training events. Even as simple a gesture as a signature file with a mission statement can enhance a service presentation.

Information Management as Asset Management

Knowledge-intensive organizations are increasingly managing information technology and content together as information assets. Knowledge accumulated by an organization in the course of its work may be represented in libraries, publications, documents, files, archives, databases, maps, or the minds of its staff. An organization, whatever its purpose, whose success depends on the ability of its staff to apply accumulated knowledge to new work, must be able to manage these assets for instant availability to anyone on the staff needing access to some necessary element.(7) "Information access" in this environment requires a new wholistic approach to this variety of resources, informed with understanding of their meaning to their users. This possibility is a comparative advantage that special librarians can seize. The technical basis learned in library school: cataloging, database searching, thesaurus building, programming, and so on, are necessary elements. But alone they are no longer enough to become a manager of information assets.

POINTERS FOR ACHIEVING SUCCESS

I believe that the information world would on the whole benefit from librarians educated in programs more analagous to the MBA or MPA in that the emphasis is on cultivating management, analytic, and problem-solving skills for graduates at the professional level, while it is assumed that the technical tasks will be done by specialized support staff. Of course, perhaps MLS programs have changed in the same 12 years that I have.

Specific knowledge and skills that I have found absolutely necessary include the following.

● Service management principles and techniques adapted from industry.

● Service marketing knowledge, skills, and survey research methods developed in the for-profit sector and adapted for nonprofits. Analytic thinking and problem solving skills matter most in this area.

● Interpersonal communication skills for using helping interviewing techniques in reference work. Empathic and teaching skills matter most in this area, such that each reference encounter can be turned into a satisfactory and pleasurable learning experience for the user.

● Mass communication skills for using e-mail and publications effectively within an organization, such that users are encouraged and supported in successful information-seeking.

● Management communication skills for capturing and representing service values in economic, statistical, graphic, visionary, or whatever terms most appeal to and are most easily understood by one's own management and stakeholders.

● Information technology and systems skills sufficient to know what one needs the systems to do, so that one can procure or design what is needed, and can extract the right technical support from the computer technical staff on the one hand and necessary resources from management on the other.

REFERENCES

1. Berry, Leonard L.; Zeithaml, Valarie; Parasuraman, A. Five imperatives for improving service quality. *Sloan Management Review.* 29-38; 1990 Summer.
(The authors' research findings were reported in a series of articles published in the *Journal of Marketing* between 1985 and 1988.)
2. Levitt, Theodore. Marketing intangible products and product intangibles. *Harvard Business Review.* 94-102; 1981 May-June.   A classic on the subject.
(The authors' research findings were reported in a series of articles published in the *Journal of Marketing* between 1985 and 1988.)

3. MacMullin, Susan E.; Taylor, Robert S. Problem dimensions and information traits. *The Information Society.* 3 : 91-113; 1984.

(The authors' research findings were reported in a series of articles published in the *Journal of Marketing* between 1985 and 1988.)

4. Taylor, Robert S. Question negotiation and information seeking in libraries. *College & Research Libraries.* 29(3): 78-94; 1968.

(The authors' research findings were reported in a series of articles published in the *Journal of Marketing* between 1985 and 1988.)

5. Dervin, Brenda. Information as a user construct: the relevance of perceived information needs to synthesis and interpretation. In: Ward, Spencer, ed. *Knowledge structure and use.* Philadelphia: Temple University Press; 1983: 155-183.

(The authors' research findings were reported in a series of articles published in the *Journal of Marketing* between 1985 and 1988.)

6. Barlow, John Perry. A taxonomy of information. *Bulletin of the American Society for Information Science.* 13-17; 1994 June/July.

(The authors' research findings were reported in a series of articles published in the *Journal of Marketing* between 1985 and 1988.)

7. Senge, Peter M. *The fifth discipline: the art and practice of the learning organization.* New York: Doubleday; 1990.

(The authors' research findings were reported in a series of articles published in the *Journal of Marketing* between 1985 and 1988.)

Jeanne Tifft
AAMC Librarian
Association of American Medical Colleges
2450 N St NW
Washington DC 20037-1127
Telephone: 202/828-0550; Fax: 202/828-1123
E-mail: jtifft@aamc.org

Part Four
Analytical Study

CHAPTER 21

EVOLVING ROLES OF HEALTH SCIENCES LIBRARIANS: A PRELIMINARY REPORT

JANA BRADLEY
Applied Informatics/UMLS Fellow,
National Library of Medicine

INTRODUCTION

The need for new roles, new skills, and new partnerships has been a theme in the literature of the health science librarianship for more than a decade. (1)(2)(3)(4)(5)(6)(7)(8). In increasing numbers, health science librarians are responding to the changes in the health domain and in health information by assuming new roles. The purpose of this chapter is to summarize briefly the results of a study of evolving roles for health science librarians that I have undertaken as part of a grant from the National Library of Medicine, given to the University of Illinois (Linda C. Smith, Principal Investigator). The study was intended to add to an understanding of the changes that are taking place in the careers of health science librarians and the implications of these changes for educating future library and information science professionals.

Study of Innovative Roles

The study solicited descriptions of innovative roles from librarians working in the field. More than fifty responses were received. A preliminary report of some of these roles has appeared (9), and a full report of the study is in preparation. Respondents were self-selected and therefore represent librarians who perceived their work as different from traditional library work. Their responses were analyzed and grouped into four categories: 1) innovations in the nature of the work performed within the umbrella of library services, 2) expanded institutional roles, 3) outreach to new clientele, and 4) positions outside libraries.

NATURE OF THE WORK

On closer examination, many new activities are extensions, in one direction or another, of established activities of LIS professionals. Providing access to electronic information resources is becoming a major activity. Health sciences libraries develop CD-ROM networks for both electronic bibliographic databases, such as Medline, and increasingly full text, commercially available electronic resources on local CD-ROM networks. They provide access to Internet resources, particularly the World Wide Web, and are becoming their institution's experts in locating web information.

Moving beyond provision of access and reference services using the web, web pages provided by libraries are interesting examples of a combination of new activities. The web page itself is an electronic publication, and, when well done, illustrates the librarians' skill in electronic information design. Library web pages usually provide a wealth of information about the library, its staff and policies, thus illustrating the public relations and information function of web pages. A primary function of health science library web pages is to organize the chaotic world of Web information for library users by providing linked lists of useful resources in a wide variety of specialty areas. Libraries are also collaborating to extend the subject coverage of web resources in projects such as the HealthWeb, originally sponsored by the libraries of the Consortium on Institutional Cooperation and now in the process of extending participation to additional libraries. Web pages are increasingly becoming extenders of the library without walls, not only by providing gateways to databases and full text resources on local or global networks, but also by providing forms-based access to services.

The library's new role as a publisher of electronic products deserves special attention. The web is increasingly being used to deliver these products. Products vary widely. Some examples are JEDI (Jefferson Electronic Documentary Images) at the Scott Library, Thomas Jefferson University; and the web-based HIV/AIDS information resource at the Active Digital Library, a part of the Erskine Medical Library at Vanderbilt.

Another area where health sciences LIS professionals are extending their activities is related to instruction and teaching. Long involved in teaching electronic searching, instructional content provided by librarians is expanding to include information management, use of information systems, networking, and networked resources, computer literacy, and other subjects related to electronic information. Librarians are also moving beyond the library to play active roles in curriculum restructuring and resource design. At Tufts University, the health sciences staff is integrating and digitizing the syllabi and lecture and lab slides and storing them as indexed searchable documents for the first two years of medical school. The veterinary school and the dental school are also contributing to this database. The library staff at the Countway Library at Harvard works with faculty to move their courses onto Web-based platforms. Some courses, for example Cell Biology 201, are now taught in the Countway in their new Knowledge Lab.

Health sciences library staff at the University of North Carolina regularly consult with faculty about the incorporation of computers and information technology into their teaching and about the development of courseware. At the Edward G. Miner Library at the University of Rochester, the library, in collaboration with Medical Informatics, developed a credentialing program in informatics for medical students, and the library is responsible for implementing it. The Dana Medical Library at the University of Vermont has been given responsibility for a Vertical Curriculum in Information Literacy and Applied Medical Informatics spanning the four years of undergraduate medical education. Virtually all of the library's faculty (MLS's) teach with MDs in the core clerkships and other health professions school, and most have joint appointments in their disciplines.

Expanded Institutional Roles

A major theme in many descriptions of new roles is the greater involvement of the librarian in institutional activities beyond the library. Numerous health sciences librarians are active in developing and providing electronic information products for their institution or organization. For example, the librarian at the Maricopa Medical Center is the webmaster for the hospital's website, as well as for the library's home page. He is developing the library's home page as the primary access point within the institution to electronic knowledge-based information systems. The library at the University of Virginia's Health Sciences Center is the coordinating body for the Center's web pages. The Lister Hill Library at the University of Alabama is involved in technology management for the institution by supporting and maintaining its World Wide Web server. Numerous hospital librarians are becoming the web experts for their institutions and are involved with, often with primary responsibility for, web pages and the development of intranets.

Countway Library at Harvard actively supports electronic publications and products produced by its varied clientele. They work with faculty to mount databases, such as the Whole Brain Atlas. They have contracts for putting up electronic publications for various organizations, and they manage gene sequencing software tools for the medical school.

As librarians have gained credibility in the area of electronic information management, they have assumed expanded roles in planning, policy development, and project leadership in their institutions and organizations. Many hospital librarians serve on information management committees, and both hospital and academic librarians are often major players on web and Internet policy committees, information systems and policy advisory committees, and other policy bodies concerned with electronic information. Librarians are also playing various roles in telemedicine outreach, including several who are in institution-wide project leadership roles.

Within their institutions, numerous librarians are assuming new areas of responsibility, in addition to their library activities. At Columbia Hospital, Milwaukee, Wisconsin, the Director of Library Services, a librarian, is also the Manager of Coordinated Care, working with multidisciplinary teams to develop clinical pathways for selected populations. At Kootenai Medical Center in Coeur d'Alene, Idaho, the librarian is the Library Services and Grants Development Manager, and researches and develops grant proposals for the hospital.

New institutional entities are also emerging, with the library as a part. For example, at the Wyoming Medical Center, in Casper, Wyoming, the library is now part of the Information Services department, contributing its skills to the IS team effort.

Librarians also assume roles for the management of these larger units. The newly created Information Management Service at the Medical Center, Department of Veterans Affairs, Biloxi, Mississippi, is headed by a librarian as chief information officer. The new department includes the resources and functions of the computer department, medical records, libraries, telecommunications, publications, and clinical staff responsible for implementing the electronic medical record. At the Levy Library, Mount Sinai School of Medicine, the library, Academic Computing and Computer Assisted Instruction are one unit managed by the librarian. Academic Information Services and Research, at Thomas Jefferson University, includes the library, academic computing, and medical media services and employs a diverse team of professionals, including librarians, computer scientists, graphics artists, and other media, health and educational professionals. AISR is under the direction of the university librarian.

Outreach to New Clientele

Innovation also occurs when librarians and libraries extend services to previously underserved or unserved clientele. Networking technology often facilitates the provision of distributed services. At the University of North Carolina, the health sciences library is rethinking its approach to distance service in order to meet the needs of the growing community-based education faculty, staff, and students. At Suburban Hospital in Bethesda, Maryland, the librarian visits physicians in their offices and demonstrates Medline, bibliographic reference management software, CD-ROMs, the Internet, and the hospital's information system. The Rural Health Village, VTEMDNET, is a project serving the state, coordinated and managed by the librarians at the Dana Medical Library in Vermont. The health information resources pages designed for the general public on Michigan Electronic Library (MEL), are maintained by a health sciences librarian. Public health workers are another example of an underserved population that is now receiving attention from health sciences librarians, often by the provision of distributed or electronic services.

Positions Outside Libraries

Innovative roles discussed so far have been undertaken by librarians employed within the structure of traditional libraries. Arguably, the largest area for job market growth exists for LIS professionals using their electronic information management skills and the fundamental principles of librarianship translated for information in general, in non-library settings. A small but important number of LIS professionals have worked in non-library settings in the past, but with the burgeoning demand for electronic information management skills, the opportunities may be predicted to grow. Obtaining jobs that are not earmarked for LIS professionals still relies, as it always did, on the professional's ability to sell the importance of his/her skills to the setting of choice. With the increased visibility of electronic information resources, this may become easier. Many new library school graduates are already finding that their World Wide Web skills interest employers greatly, and that opportunities to use their general information management skills follow.

Several examples illustrate different types of non-library settings. Self-employed librarians, working as information brokers or as circuit-riding librarians, are early examples of health sciences librarians working from noninstitutional settings. Two librarians work in the Health Information Unit of the Department of Clinical Epidemiology and Biostatistics of the Faculty of Health Sciences at McMaster University. Their jobs include research, teaching Medline, and writing and producing two health care journals.

Serving as a corporate information specialist outside a library setting is also a growing role. Work can vary from project to project and include research and report writing as well as traditional activities. At Amgen Incorporated an LIS professional has developed and manages an online library of outside meetings, meeting reports, industry news, position papers, key references, and other information vital to the company.

SUMMARY

In conclusion, a few general comments about innovative roles for LIS professionals can be ventured. New roles almost always involve information technology, and value the LIS professional's skills and knowledge in technology management. However, the LIS professional's ability to manage electronic information—to know how to find it, evaluate it, and use it—is the core value for many of these roles. The technology is highly visible at the moment, but the information, albeit in electronic form, is the true star.

LIS professionals often succeed in their new roles because of what might be called, metaskills. Examples of such metaskills might be collaborative ability, the ability to negotiate and balance competitive interests, listening ability, and the ability to tease real information needs out of a complex situation. And finally, roles evolve, and one thing leads to another.

REFERENCES

Footnotes
[1] The study was part of a grant to the University of Illinois from the National Library of Medicine, Linda C. Smith, principal investigator.

Endnotes
(1). Anderson, Rachel. Reinventing the medical librarian. *Bulletin of the Medical Library Association*. 77: 323-331; 1989 Oct.
(2). Braude, Robert M. Impact of information technology on the role of

the health sciences librarian. *Bulletin of the Medical Library Association.* 81: 408-413; 1993 Oct.

(3). Florance, Valerie; Matheson, Nina. The health sciences librarian as knowledge worker. *Library Trends.* 42: 196-219; 1993.

(4). Bradley, Jana., The changing face of health information and health information work. *Bulletin of the Medical Library Association.* 84: 1-10; 1996 January.

(5). Frisse, Mark; Braude, Robert; Florance, Valerie; Fuller, Sherrilynn. Informatics and medical libraries: changing needs and changing roles. *Academic Medicine.* 70: 30-35; 1995.

(6). Matheson, Nina. The idea of the library in the 21st century. *Bulletin of the Medical Library Association.* 83:1-7; 1995 January.

(7). Bradley, Jana. Management of information: an analysis of the Joint Commission's standards for information management. *Topics in Health Information Management.* 16: 51-63; 1965 November.

(8). Broering, Naomi. High performance medical libraries. *Advances in information management for the virtual era.* Westport, CT: Meckler; 1993.

(9). Bradley, Jana. Pioneers in information territory. Presidential address; 1996. *Bulletin of the Medical Library Association.* 85: 1997 January.

Jana Bradley
Applied Informatics:UMLS Fellow,
National Library of Medicine, and
Indiana University School of Library and Information Science
on the IUPUI campus (on leave)
Tel: 317/251-3779; Fax: 317/278-1807
E-mail: bradley@velcome.iupui.edu

Part Five

Index

INDEX